A MILLION MILES AGO,
THE JOURNEY CONTINUES

A MILLION MILES AGO, THE JOURNEY CONTINUES

MAE BLACK BUCKEL

A MILLION MILES AGO, THE JOURNEY CONTINUES

iUniverse books may be ordered through booksellers or by contacting:

iUniverse LLC
1663 Liberty Drive
Bloomington, IN 47403
www.iuniverse.com
1-800-Authors (1-800-288-4677)

ISBN: 978-1-4917-4133-7 (sc)
ISBN: 978-1-4917-4134-4 (e)

Library of Congress Control Number: 2014912486

Printed in the United States of America.

iUniverse rev. date: 08/01/2014

REVIEWS

"Mae Black Buckel has strengths that amaze both men and women. She has borne hardships and she has carried some heavy burdens, but she holds on to happiness, love and joy. She may smile when she wants to scream. She sings when she wants to cry. Mae cries when she is happy and laughs when she feels a bit nervous. She is a fighter and stands up to injustice. Mae does not take no for an answer when there is a belief in a better solution. She has gone without so her family and others could have. She grieves at the loss of a family and yet remains strong when there is no apparent strength left. She gives hugs and kisses knowing they can heal a broken heart. The heart of Mae is what makes our world turn. She brings a fresh spirit of joy, hope and love. She is an artist who "paints" with compassion and ideas. Her words and music speak volumes as she gives moral support to her family and friends. Mae has vital things to say and everything to give. If there is a flaw in Mae, it is that she has forgotten her value and worth to all of us who read and listens to her God given talent. Carl Snodgrass, CDRUSN Ret.

"I just want to congratulate you on your new life. Ms. Mae from the first day I met you, I knew you were special. You are a jewel and a treasure to your family. After reading your book *A Million Miles Ago,* I was amazed at how God kept you through it all. I know that your book will be an inspiration to all of God's children that read your story. I believe that God will use your book to bless other women and your story will teach others that, *Joy cometh in the morning.* Peace and blessings to you. Vandra Parks, Health Connect America, Memphis, Tennessee

"Well, I first would like to say that your book was very inspiring, motivating and very real. I took so much from reading it. From the genuine love, a mother has for her children to the love and faithfulness one carries and displays to her husband and the faith that you had in our Lord and Savior Jesus Christ. I have recently struggled with several obstacles that I knew in my heart I would need to settle at some point. I honestly reflected back on my life, began to take several of the readings and scriptures, and began to see how if I trust in God and pray for guidance in forgiving others he would show me.

He forgave me and I must forgive others. I wanted to forgive. How do I help these babies and guide them the way you would have me to Lord, loving them no matter their choices. In A *Million Miles Ago*, you painted a vision of a mother that did what it took to take care of your children and family, loving beyond all bad choices. Your love and faithfulness to the Lord Jesus Christ is genuine and clearly understood. I found this book to have helped me in those ways and so many more. Thank you, Ms. Mae for making it simple and truthful.

Ginny Lynn Corum Smith

INTRODUCTION

In the following pages you will read about a woman born in the rural South near the end of the Depression. A woman abused and exploited as a child and as an adult, a woman who was saved by the blood of Christ.

This book is a book of praise and thanksgiving. Yes, it details some of the painful experiences of the Author, but it is predominately a testament to the forgiveness and grace of God.

The author is not a subject of pity. Her life is witness to her strength of character and faith. God blessed her with seven children. Most of them (except one deceased) are now doing their best to get through this life in a manner that makes her and our Savior proud. You will read about physical and mental abuse heaped upon her, but pay close attention to the fact that nothing she was given to endure lessened her faith or weakened her character.

She was gifted with a wonderful voice and a talent for writing song and verse. She has been singing the praises of our Lord since childhood; she has been writing Christian songs and poetry for almost as long. After the death of her eldest son, Mae lost the inspiration and desire to write. The hiatus lasted for almost ten years. We, her readers, are glad it did not last longer.

Since taking up the pin again, Mae has written volumes of poetry and Gospel music. Several of her poems have won International recognition. Many of her songs have received airplay here in the United States and in many other countries over the world. Her first book of poems, Inspirations has made an impact on all who have read it. The book has been used in prison outreach programs. It has also been circulated among our troops overseas and has become suggested reading in churches and hospitals in many areas of our country.

I was Mae's pastor for almost 7 years and our friendship continues to this day. Mae's children were very young and life was very difficult for them during those years. She struggled, but continued to trust God when her faith was tested. She came to church and brought her children, faithfully. She was a member of the church choir and sang specials also. Mae loved to worship God.

She had a hard life but was always soft spoken and had a kind and gentle spirit. Her deep faith in God kept her spirit sweet."

Pastor Willard Gardner, Russellville Church of God, Russellville, Tennessee

FOREWORD

When I first met Mae, she referred me to her web site where, she said, you can learn all about Mae Black. Upon reading a reading of the first five or six of her poems, I knew I had to get to know this woman of God.

It is in God's word that, out of the abundance of the heart, the lips speak. The gift that God has given Mae to write poetry that reflects his glory and the majesty of Jesus Christ was not misplaced.

Every precious stone and all metals come from the earth formed by the hand of God. Emeralds, Sapphires, Diamonds, Rubies, Opals, Silver, Gold, Tin, Copper, Platinum, {and many other metals}, the earth from where they are extracted, differs only in the mineral content. One important commonality, these precious stones and metals are formed, and created by heat and pressure. Mae has experienced an incredible difficult life. She has certainly experienced heat and pressure. With life sustaining strength and anointing of our Lord and Savior Jesus Christ, Mae has come through all these trials as a precious jewel of the Lord Jesus Christ and is more than fit for his use.

Mae writes about the Lord yes, but also about the sin-sick condition of the world, we live in and she does so from a perspective of how God must see things. Mae has a heart of great compassion for her fellow man and especially for our fighting men and women. She writes about the difficult conditions that these wonderful warriors find themselves in.

There is nothing pretentious about Mae. Her capability to minister salvation, restoration, healing and a brand new life as the reader is introduced to the living God, the Lord Jesus Christ. Mae makes it abundantly clear that there is a loving Savior; waiting to embrace and forgive every person who desires a new life in Him. As has often been said, God is good! And a reading of this book will be an encouragement to you and all you share it with.

Rev, Don Buckel, Administrative Assistant

ACKNOWLEDGEMENTS

I give thanks first to Jesus Christ, without whom there would be no words or reason for this book. I then give thanks to the following people who have been, at some point in my life, a blessing and inspiration, a friend or the hand that God used to help me through the storms of my life. They have seen my tears and pain, my trials and my triumphs. To name them all would be impossible, for my friends are countless.

To my late husband, Don Buckel, who taught me that dreams do come true.
To my children and their father who, walked with me there.
To the Buckel family for all the joys they have brought into my life.
To my grandchildren, who is my sunshine.
To Rev. Willard and Patsy Gardner who grounded, me in faith.
To my lifelong friend Erma Williamson who, picked me up more than once.
To Quinn and Jewel Williams and family, who helped me to keep on the right path.
To Vandra Parks, Health Connect America, for her hands extended beyond the call of duty in difficult times.
To Rev. William and Opel Newton, Rev. James and Peggy Newton, who walked me to the cross and introduced me to Jesus Christ.
To the Clarksdale Church of God for love and fellowship 1965-1989.
To Jim and Elaine Sanders, who stuck it out until the victory came.
My son-in-laws, Billy Anderson and Steve Barnhart, who have given me love and support in difficult times.
To my song publishers, Edward King EHK Music, and Barbara Dunn, for promoting my music over the airways.
To Loman Craig of Bandit Records, Jeff Stone of Empire Music Company and the Hit City Singers, for the beautiful work done on my music.
To Edward and Mirrell High, who made me, laugh when there was no reason to laugh.
To my daughter-in-law, Debbie Lawson Black for the work she did editing my manuscript.
To our military men and women, who fight for my freedom to express my thoughts.
To all of you, I give thanks!

Chapter 1

THE BEGINNING

(All scriptures in this book taken from
King James Version of the Bible)

I was born Era Mae Taylor, January nineteen, nineteen thirty-eight, close to midnight, in an old country house near Alligator, Mississippi. I was the third child of six added to my family. I never knew why they gave me this name. I was called Era Mae all of my life until I married and left home. I then dropped the Era and became Mae. My entrance into the world was not an easy thing for my mother, having only a midwife and a kerosene lamp and no proper equipment. I can only imagine the pain she suffered giving me life.

I would be two years old when we entered the forties. This would begin a decade of hardships and heartbreak for our country. In the middle of trying to recover from the great depression, we had the attack on Pearl Harbor and then World War II. I was just a toddler and understood nothing about world problems, War, Nazis, Adolf Hitler, or the Holocaust. My biggest concern then was if my mom would pick me up if I cried.

Things were hard all over the country, but harder in the Mississippi Delta and other Southern States; a time when many men would be away at war and families left to struggle just to get by. Farmers worked long hours for little pay just to feed their families. It was a time of racial prejudice and unrest between the blacks and the whites, and more so in the South. It would take many years for some to realize that all men should be equal and that God meant all men to be free. We have come a long way in my lifetime, yet many still have not learned that all men have a right to freedom, and no one is exempt from God's love.

We were poor but mother always managed to keep us fed and warm. In addition to working in the fields, she raised a garden in the summer for vegetables. She raised chickens for meat and eggs and most of the time we had a cow for milk and butter. Mother would milk the cow and then she would divide the milk into two containers, one for drinking and the other for the buttermilk. She would let the milk for butter sit overnight in a churn, until it clabbered. Then she would churn the milk until butter formed on top. She would then skim off the butter, place it in a mold and let it cool in the icebox, and then we had fresh butter, most of the time. She used the buttermilk for baking biscuits and cornbread.

In the winter, my dad would kill a hog and we would have ham, sausage, bacon, pork roast or plain fried pork. The icebox was a thing that looked like a refrigerator, but daddy had to buy fifty-pound blocks of ice to put in it to make it cold. In the summer, he bought a lot of ice. Back then, they sold flour in twenty-five pound cotton bags with different kinds of print on them, such as flowers or rainbows. Mother would use the bags to make us dresses. She made sure we had two dresses each. She also made sure one or the other dresses were clean for school each day. She hand stitched our dresses until my grandpa gave her an old sewing machine.

Mother did our laundry in an outside washtub with a scrub board. She would heat the smoothing iron on the old wood burning cook stove and iron out the wrinkles. I remember helping her do the laundry when I had to stand on a box to reach over the tub. She would scrub the clothes on the rub-board until her hands would be chaffed and sore. It was hard work, but I do not remember mother ever complaining about anything.

Sometimes in the winter, the old house would be very cold because the fire in the fireplace would go out during the night. Mother would put us girls in bed with her to keep us warm, and then she would put my brothers in a bed together so they could keep each other warm. Many times, she would have to go into the woods to find tree limbs and scrap wood to keep the fire burning in the fireplace.

Daddy was a farmer, but he did other things too. If a car or truck needed repair he was a mechanic; if someone needed a haircut, he was a barber, but mostly he was a farmer. He was a sharecropper, which meant, he would work a few acres of land for half the profits. We never saw much profit because by the time harvest rolled around, the company store had eaten it up.

Daddy may have been a good man at one time, but he liked to drink. After a few years hitting the bottle, he seemed to take on two different personalities: when he was sober; he was just mean; when he was drunk, he was vicious. He bought an old truck; the kind you had to start by turning a crank. When he would get thirsty, he would have to go into town to get a bottle of whisky. Sometimes he would be so drunk by the time he finally made it home, he would pass out in the truck. Mother and my older brother would get him inside, put him to bed and then she would cry. We never did understand how daddy could find his way back home without getting himself killed. He would be too drunk to stand on his feet, yet he could drive that vehicle over those curved and bumpy country roads. Mother would always say God takes care of drunks and fools.

We never had electricity or inside plumbing, so we pumped all our water by hand from a water pump. Most country people of that time did the same. The pump was a long pipe driven into the ground until it rested in an underground pool of water or a stream. We would pump the water into buckets and then bring it inside to use. My older brother, two years older than I, usually had to do most of the water pumping when he got old enough. He would work all day in the fields, and then pump the water needed for use in the kitchen and for the rest of us to take baths. In the summer we would let the water sit in the sunshine all day so it would be warm for our baths at night. In the winter, we heated the water on the old wood burning stove my mother used for cooking. With no electricity, we had no such thing as a hot water heater. Life was hardest on my brother because he had to do most of the chores, and during the winter months, he cut wood for the stove and the fireplace. The rest of us would gather wood and bring in the water. My brother cut all the wood with an axe, because there was no such thing as a chain saw or at least we never heard of one. When my brother got old enough, he started driving a tractor and plowing the fields, but he still had to do his regular chores after he finished the plowing. When I look back, I know he had the hardest growing up of all of us.

Chapter 2

THE COTTON FIELDS

As far back as I can remember we all worked in the fields, chopping cotton in the spring, picking it in the summer and fall. When we were little, we would follow mother down the cotton rows with little sacks she had made out of flour bags. When our little sacks got full, we would dump them into mother's big bag. As soon as we were big enough, we would have our own cotton sack. The sack had a strap that looped over the head so we would have both hands free to pick and to drag the sack at the same time. When the sack was full, it weighed about 100 pounds. If there was cotton left in the fields when the weather got cold, daddy would pull it off the stalks, bring it inside the house and then we would pick the cotton to keep it from going to waste.

You do not know what you have missed if you have never worked in a cotton field! You missed getting up before daylight, going to the fields by sunrise, taking an hour break for a little lunch, then returning to work until sunset. You missed your clothes being wet from top to bottom from the morning dew. They would dry in the heat of the sun but become just as wet from sweat as the day wore on. The work was hard, but there was a kind of beauty to it; or maybe I was the only one who saw it that way. We all worked five days a week. Daddy would not allow us to work on Saturday or Sunday, so we could just be kids on the weekends.

As a little girl, I would watch the men walk behind the cotton planter, pulled by two mules, planting the seeds in the black earth. We would watch the seeds sprout, then turn into a field of sturdy green stalks. Soon the stalks would bud and open into white, pink, purple and yellow flowers. There would be acres and acres of green stalks, adorned with colors of the rainbow. When the flowers wilted and fell off the stalks the green bolls would take their place. Soon they would open to snow white cotton. As far as could be seen, the fields would look as if covered in snow. It was breathtakingly beautiful. When the harvest was over, daddy would settle with the boss. If there were any profit left, he would let mother order new clothes from the Sears and Roebuck catalogue. We knew that whatever she ordered had to last us until the next harvest.

We received hand-me-downs from our teachers and some of the richer kids at our school. We were thankful for everything we had, so we were grateful, but we were still too proud to wear clothes to school that someone else had worn the year before, at least I was. I would save my hand-me-downs for the weekends.

A few years later, progress would come to the cotton fields with the introduction of the mechanical cotton picking machine. In the eyes of the farmers of the time, all the new marvel did was make a mess of the fields, leaving valuable cotton to rot and many farm workers without jobs.

THE COTTON FIELDS

For Christmas, we would all get stockings filled with candy, an apple, orange and some nuts. The stockings were the whole of our presents, but we were happy to get them. What toys we had, we made ourselves. The boys would make toy guns from sticks or tom-walkers from tin cans. They made the walkers by cutting holes on each side of the can and pulling a wire through the holes. They could walk, then, by stepping up on the cans using the wire for a handle.

The girls would cut out paper dolls and things from the Sears catalogue. We would cut out men, women, kids, toys, furniture, dishes and all kinds of things. Then we would make paste by mixing water and flour and use it for glue to paste all the wonderful things together for our pretty paper house. We would sit for hours arranging and pasting it all together and enjoy our little dream world.

We sometimes lived on farms where other families lived; and it was normal for all the men in the area to gather at our house for haircuts, because my dad was a barber. Sometimes they would bring beer and whisky, get drunk and end up run off the place by my mother, after daddy passed out from too many drinks. Times were bad and the work was hard, but we learned valuable lessons that would help us in later years. We learned to appreciate what we had and we learned that work was the way to get what we wanted. We learned that there were no free lunches.

Chapter 3

GROWING PAINS

This was a time in my life when I was very young and confused about many things. As we worked in the fields, sometimes, side by side with people of different color, we were white and they were black. We could play outside together and work together, but we had separate schools and churches and lived in separate parts of town. I grew up in an environment of racial bigotry and hatred towards people because of the color of their skin. I hated it, and wondered why it was that way. I remember a sweet elderly black woman who lived near us on one of the farms we worked. I would go to her house and sit on her porch. She would give me candy bars. She would tell me stories about her life and her childhood. I felt bad that I had no present to give her after she was so nice to me.

Wildflowers would grow in the woods or on the roadsides and sometimes I would stop and pick buttercups and honeysuckles for her. She would tell me I was a sweet child and that she would pray for me every day. I am sure she did just that. I did not know she should not be my friend. Poor children saw no difference between themselves. Color was not important to children. We were all poor, we all worked very hard and we all faced the same daily struggles. When I get to Heaven, I will find this friend and let her know that God answered her prayers. I never forgot her kindness, and it did not matter that she was black and I was white. However, prejudice does not stop with race or religion, or nationalities; it goes deeper into the heart of man, and eats away at the soul like a cancer. I have always been thankful that God gave me a mother with a Godly love in her heart, who taught me that to look down on others because they are different and less fortunate than I, is sin.

When we were little kids, it did not matter that we were poor. We did not know we were poor. Most of those around us were in the same circumstances. Being poor did not make an impression on me until I discovered I did not dress like many of the other little girls in school. I was very shy and did not make friends easily. I became shyer because of my feelings of being different.

There were two schools in our area, one for whites and the other for blacks. All the white kids went to the same school, rich and poor alike;

the black kids went to a different school. The poorer children would take sack lunches and eat at their desk or in the schoolyard. The richer children would eat in the cafeteria, the two groups seldom mingled. Just as in the old story, we did walk miles to the bus stop. Some days I thought my feet would freeze because the soles of my shoes flapped as I walked. We did homework by kerosene lamp light. I loved school, but we could only go to classes in the winter, between crop seasons. I managed to make decent grades, but it was hard for all of us to keep up when we missed more school than we attended. There were no laws back then to force us to go, so I dropped out in the eighth grade, many kids dropped out of school back then for the same reasons. My dream of graduating and making a better life for myself was lost. We had to pick up what education we could after we were grown.

We moved around a lot, wherever daddy could find work. The new place was never far from the last one, so we did not have to change schools, and our friends stayed the same.

The biggest town I saw while I was growing up in the Mississippi Delta had a service station, a post office, a bank, a movie theater, a train station and a few stores and churches. Sometimes daddy would take us there on Saturday afternoon to see a movie. We could stay from opening until closing at midnight. We could get a ticket, a bag of popcorn, a candy bar and a soda all for thirty-five cents. We could watch a double feature, Tarzan and Jane, Roy Rodgers and Dale Evans, Hop-a-long Cassidy, the Jungle Girl or the Lone Ranger, all for one price.

We stayed at the theater all afternoon and evening because daddy would be across the tracts, drinking and gambling with his friends. When closing time came, my older brother would have to find our father, drag him into the old truck or car, whichever vehicle we had at the time and drive us home. My mother and brother would get him inside and into bed, many times, without waking him up. If he awakened, there would be more hell to pay for all of us, but my mother paid most of it. When daddy was sober, he was hard to live with, but when he drank whisky, he was hell on wheels; as a result, mother had a hard life raising six kids. When he drank, we knew to stay out of his way and we knew not to cross him. I think we really loved him, but the fear always got in the way.

Chapter 4
FOND MEMORIES

God gives us friends in life to help us through the bad times and rejoice with us in the good times. Sometimes he sends us playmates when we are children to share our little world. It is such a blessing to be able to keep those friends all through our lives.

There was such a family, which was very special to us. They stayed close to us all of our growing up years. If we moved to a different farm, they moved there also. There were five kids in their family, four boys and one girl. The ages of the children in their family were close to our own ages and we became like brothers and sisters instead of just friends. We always found some kind of entertainment for ourselves. We did not have television, Internet, games or cell phones. We did not even have a house phone. Imagine that! We played hide and seek, softball, climbing trees or just roaming the countryside, looking for bugs or whatever. The boys took great pleasure in making the girls feel silly. One of the things they thought was the funniest thing ever was to put one of the girls inside an old tire, give the tire a shove and let it roll over and over until it rolled into the side of the house or a tree. When the girl got out, she would stagger around like a drunk and the boys would laugh and laugh.

No matter where we lived, there were always creeks, woods, ditches and a river nearby. Mother never had to worry about us getting into trouble, as there was nothing for us to get into, except kid stuff. She did not worry about anyone bothering us on the creek or in the woods because no one ever went there except us kids. However, our parents never knew how daring we kids were and the danger we placed ourselves in while playing some of our little games.

During that time, the government started putting pipelines through the country areas. A river ran near our friends' house. The pipeline workers had to stretch cables across the river so they could cross back and forth because there was no bridge. They had to string two cables, one over the other, far enough apart for the pipeline worker to step on the bottom cable, hold on to the top cable and walk across the river. Occasionally, our parents would go into town for supplies on Saturdays. They would leave us in care of the two older boys. By this time, the older boys in that family were in their late teens. On one of those Saturdays, the boys said they would take us (my sister, my friend and I) for a canoe ride across the river and back.

They paddled us across the river and left us. They told us if we wanted to get back across, we had to swim or walk the cable. Not one of us knew how to swim and walking the cable seemed terrifying, but we knew we had best go back home before our parents returned. The decision was not hard. My sister and our friend were older and taller than I was. They could reach both cables fine, but I was little and could barely reach the top cable. I can still see that water swirling every time I looked down, as I inched my way back across the river. I screamed all the way across while the boys just roared with laughter. I swore to myself, if I ever get big enough, I would pay them back good. We knew our parents would be home soon when we heard the old car coming down the road. The boys threatened to throw all of us in the river next time, if we told on them. We never said a word.

There was a ditch behind our house, which was very deep. In the summer, it would be dry and we would play in it. The boys would make sleds from old boards by tying ropes to them. They would pull us up and down the banks of the ditch. In the winter, when it rained, the ditch would fill up and spill over. Daddy nailed some boards together to make a bridge so he could drive his truck across and he anchored the bridge with rope to keep it from floating away. We were not supposed to go near the ditch when it rained in the winter.

One winter day it started raining and continued for about a week. Of course, the ditch spilled over and the little bridge was floating. We girls decided to sneak out and watch the water as it rolled by. My baby sister was four and I was seven. The other two girls were a bit older. We got to the ditch and thought we would step on the bridge, just to see if it would move. Suddenly the bridge tilted and my baby sister tumbled head first into the churning water. We grabbed her by her feet and pulled her out. I believe she was close to drowning. We ran back to the house, scared half to death, little sister nearly frozen. We just knew daddy would kill all of us. We told mother what happened. I think because she was so grateful we had not drowned her baby girl, she never told daddy. We needed a whipping for that one and we knew it. We never went near that ditch again when it rained, even a sprinkle.

At that time, I had only one younger brother who was just a toddler. Our last brother was yet to be born. My little sister was always tagging along with us older kids and we were supposed to take care of her. We nicknamed her Tag-a-long-too-Lou. There was a barn in our friend's yard, which had a loft, for hay storage. The chickens would go up in the loft and lay eggs. Sometimes we would go up there to gather the eggs. One day, we older girls went up to the loft and my younger sister followed. There was an opening in front of the barn loft. We intended to make a game of gathering the eggs by throwing them down through the opening and the boys would catch them before they hit the ground. Little Tag-a-long-too-Lou went to the edge of the opening to look down, lost her balance and fell. The distance from the loft opening to the ground was like a two story building. Instead of catching eggs, the boys caught my little sister, just before she hit the ground. Thank God!

Farmers use to pile their hay in stacks. The stacks were very high, like big domes. The older boys would climb to the top of the haystacks, taking an old tire with them. The other kids would do a dance around the hay while the boys would throw the tires down, trying to hook us, but we always got away before our necks got broken.

We climbed trees, rolled in tires, played in the ditches, and did many things that were dangerous for us. We nearly drove our mothers crazy. Today's mothers worry about drugs, gangs, shootings, sexual promiscuity and sexually transmitted diseases.

The family I mentioned earlier plus a few more farmers who lived in the area came to visit often. The men would listen to the fights or the news on the battery-powered radio, and the wives would visit over coffee or tea. All the children between the two families, there were lots of them, would play outside. The older boys seemed to watch over all of us little girls. We were like sisters and brothers and we trusted them.

As I look back on those years now, I do not remember ever being afraid of anything except the dark. Except for those fears, the nights would be mostly peaceful. The cotton fields and run down shacks would fade away. The sky, filled with stars that sparkled, like millions of diamonds; the moon looked as though painted on a velvet canvas. I could look out my window and make wishes on them, believing that all my wishes would come true. I did not know then, that one day all my dreams would become nightmares.

The adults would sometimes tell us that if we were not good, the boogieman would get us. I tried to be good most of the time. I did not know why there was a boogieman but I did know that there was, in fact, more than one.

Chapter 5

FEAR, CONFUSION AND SHAME

This chapter is very difficult for me to write. I have prayed much about including it. I did not desire to go back to these memories. I did not want to revisit painful occurrences that I never told anyone about, not even those closest to me. The Lord was merciful by erasing those memories from my mind until such a time that I could deal with them. I kept my silence for many years and now I ask myself, why bring it up after all these years? The Bible says that we are over comers by the blood of the Lamb and by the word of our testimony. It is only for his Glory that I can find the courage to write about them now. The world has changed so much since I was a young girl and the youth of today have not a clue as to the consequences of going against God's rules on sexual behavior.

Our society has tried to dismantle and do away with God's commandments on adultery and fornication and parents who stand on God's word are deemed as old fashion or fanatical. However, God is still the same yesterday, today and forever. He did not make his rules to place a hammer on the heads of those who break them. He made them to protect his creation from consequences of going the wrong way from his will, and he has not changed his laws to fit the times. It is my hope that I can help someone else who has suffered these things; someone, who, like me, did not know what the problem was or that his power could break the bondage of shame and confusion that one lives with in the aftermath of sexual abuse.

In my youth, sexual abuse was a subject that no one wanted to talk about and no one believed. The victims kept silent and dealt with the horror the best way they could and the rest of the world turned their heads and ignored the truth. Today the problem is so rampant that we can no longer ignore its existence. Psychiatrist offices are full of broken women and children, trying to find a way to deal with their memories of sexual abuse and the courts try to deal with the offenders.

Sexual abuse occurs in all lifestyles; from the richest to the poorest; from the ignorant to the brilliant. Sexual abuse touches kings and kingdoms, princes and presidents, preachers and pulpits, teachers and students. It has torn homes apart, caused murder and all types of addictions; it has given birth to thousands of unwanted babies; children that do not know who, nor where their parents are. Sexual abuse has also led to the abortion of countless innocent babies. No day goes by without the news media reporting more cases. Sexual abuse is international, intercultural and multilingual. The facts read like this... Every five seconds someone experiences a sexually assault. Every year in America over 680,000, women raped.

Over twelve million adult American women have been victims of forcible rape; approximately 84% of reported rapes involve an assailant known to the victim; one in five women will be the victim of a sexual assault by the time she is eighteen; one in seven men will be the victim of a sexual assault by the time he is eighteen. (Reported by the National Victims Center/Crime Victims, U. S. Senate Judiciary Committee) Is this not a sad commentary? Sexual abuse is one of the most deadly sins known to man and a sin that surely must cause pain in the heart of God.

So why did God create sex? Sex was God's gift to bless man, a physical act to consummate the commitment of a man and women exclusively to each other. God intended this gift to be sacred, private and honorable in marriage. His Word said this act would make a husband and wife one flesh. God created one man, Adam, and one woman, Eve. He gave the woman to the man. He did not make alternate partners for Adam and Eve in case they got bored with each other. The divine plan was; one man for one woman for all time. Only through death was this union to be broken. Of course, the Devil had other ideas. He sought the weakness of man's flesh that he could best use as a weapon to turn Gods blessing into a curse. The beauty that was the sex act became abused and perverted. The perversion of this gift of God has become one of the most deadly sins, causing damage to the basics of human existence.

It is an accepted fact that our country started changing in the fifties, with rape and sexual assault on the rise and by the sixties; we were feeling the thrust of change in all areas of our lives. Parents started stepping out; kids started dropping out; alcohol flowed like a river into the life of most families; illegal drugs started their epidemic spread and divorce became an accepted fact. Rock and roll music, which was sweeping the world about that time, was the culprit. Then the war in Vietnam, next the hippies took their turn at the blame game. When the blamers ran out of people to blame, they shifted the blame to whomever or whatever was available. However, domestic violence and sexual abuse did not start in the fifties, only our lack of courage to deal with these crimes kept statistics low. Rape, sexual abuse and domestic violence have been around for a long, long time. So who is to blame?

There has always been evil in the world, since Adam and Eve sinned and brought the curse down on God's creation; sexual abuse is just one of the curses. I was five years old the first time it happened to me; at least that is as far back as I can remember. I was terrified, but too young to know why I was supposed to be afraid when men touched me in a sexual way. At five years old, a child does not yet know that you cannot always trust an adult. It went on until I was big enough to fight back or run away and hide from the boogieman. I had lots of hiding places. I remember a weeping willow tree with branches that swept the ground. It became one of my favorite places. I could crawl up under its branches where no one could see me. I could then peep through the foliage to see if the boogieman was coming so I could slip out the other side and run.

I remember lying awake all night long, many nights, because I was afraid of the evil that would come through my window and grab me; sometimes I would still be awake in the morning when mother would be cooking breakfast. I would be so tired I would fall to sleep on the school bus. I was never afraid to walk in the woods or by the creek alone in the daylight, but I would head for the house when the shadows started to fall. Occasionally mother would ask me why I liked to stay in the woods so much. I would answer that I liked it because it was so peaceful and I felt safer there than anywhere else.

The nights would always bring fears. On clear nights, I could see the moon and stars from my window. I would find the Big Dipper and the Milky Way and wonder how they could be so far away when I could almost reach up and touch them. On cloudy nights, I would almost smother myself by keeping my head under the covers because I was afraid of the boogieman. I had to fight and struggle all of my growing up years to keep from being technically raped, but the rape that occurred to my mind was just as real as a physical penetration and no child should be sexually educated in that manner. I do not know how I ever got through those years without someone noticing that something was wrong. No one ever noticed.

My father was the first, but tragically, not the only man that sexually abused me as I grew up, I can remember at least four others, who were relatives or family friends. As I grew older and stronger, I could usually outwit or out kick all of them, accept my father. I was so terrified of what he would do, not only to me, but also, to all of us, especially mother. I ran when I could and survived when I could not.

I have to give a little background information here. My dear mother was the closest person to being a saint that I ever knew. She suffered and endured. She never complained. What would have been the purpose? She kept her own counsel. She loved her children above all things except God. She did the best she could with what she had. It was my love and respect for her that I never told her things that I was going through. I can only speak for my own experiences, but I am sure I was not the only little girl, back then, who suffered through the same things that I endured. We just did not talk about it. In those days, children did not know about sex, but even as a small child I knew something was wrong in what was happening to me.

I grew up feeling naked and being ashamed of my body. I was always self-conscience. It was as if I could feel someone watching me, as if being stalked. I did not realize why I felt that way. Those feelings of being exposed and the feelings of being ashamed followed me for miles down life's road. After I started school, I would shy away from the other kids. I was afraid they could see inside of me and know what was going on. I felt ashamed, but I was too young to know why I was ashamed. I was afraid to tell anyone; I did not know how to tell anyone because I did not know what was happening to me.

I felt guilty because I thought something was wrong with me, as if it was my fault, somehow. There were no child protection laws in my time, (or none that were enforced in rural Mississippi) or 911 services. Even if there had been, I would never have told anyone because of the fear and shame I carried with me all of the time.

Sadly, it is worse now than it has ever been and no child is safe. A child is born into the world an innocent. The violation of the innocent God himself will avenge in his own time.

God made us all different, with different types of personalities and different strengths and weaknesses. Each of us reacts differently to these things. In my case, it took away my self esteem and I lived all through my childhood, teen years and through a broken marriage feeling as though I was not as good as everyone else. Because I had carried those feelings around inside so long, they eventually caused me to settle for less in life than God had planned for me. I felt that I was not worthy of anything better. I pushed love away. It was as if I was trying to punish myself for what was not my fault. I carried it around bottled up inside, until it overwhelmed me. Silence led me to hate the ones who hurt me. Silence allowed those feelings that festered just below the surface to cause me to make serious mistakes, mistakes that ended up with a broken heart and a broken life.

I have heard that the young forget easily. That is not true! A child may block out bad things for a long time, but somewhere in life, the memories come back. They burn inside a person until, in many cases, they explode into violence and then we see the results of it all in a wasted life. No, a child does not forget. I still remember the bad dreams; the shadows on the wall; the hiding places; the fears of the darkness under the house, where I would hide from the hands that were going to grab me. I remember the shame; the confusion and the feelings of being soiled that carried over into my adult life. I was always afraid of dark places, yet I had to turn out lights, lock doors and I was always careful to keep my body covered no matter what. I could never get away from that self-consciousness. It was very hard to live with. Only God could free me from those emotions, and that would not come until years later.

If you are a victim of abuse, you need to tell someone! There is no help for you if you keep your silence. You have done nothing wrong! What is happening to you is not your fault! You do not have to live with the shame and guilt you feel. You do not deserve to suffer with feelings of inferiority such as I did for many, many years. It is not wrong to be poor and it is not wrong to be a victim. It is wrong not to tell someone and get help. If we do not speak out then the bad person wins, we all lose, and we end up being a victim repeatedly.

Even though we have, more laws today intended to protect the victims, when the guilty are brought before the courts, many times, they do not pay for their crime. In most cases, the defendant will go for rehabilitation for a while, and then released to commit the same acts again.

My heart goes out to the kids who are lost in this world; many are runaways. They are running from physical abuse and or sexual abuse and they are unaware that they are running to another rotten situation. They end up on the streets, trying to survive; enticed into drugs, prostitution, gangs and all manner of evil. The results can only be jail or death. We then call them criminals. Seldom do we question how they got to that point in the first place.

When a person grows up with bitterness, anger, fears and confusion in his or her heart, they have to turn to someone or something in order to cope. That is why our young people embrace drugs and become sexually promiscuous, our streets are full of gangs and our prisons are overflowing. I believe all people were born innocent and I believe we all have help getting to where we go in life, whether that life is good or bad. It is no wonder that the last words Jesus spoke from the cross was Father, forgive them, for they know not what they do. Indeed, God, help us.

If you are an abused person, no matter what form that abuse takes, you need to know, it is not your fault. You are the victim. You do not have to live in shame because evil defiled you. God is out there searching for you and if you will call his name, he will find you and come to you where you are, just as he found me. He will bind up your wounds, heal your broken heart and give you a new life. He will turn your nightmares back into dreams that you can accomplish.

Chapter 6

THE GIFT

When I was a child and even as I got older, I would go down to the creek by our house; I would sit on the bank, listen to the birds sing, play with the crawfish and in the evening, I would watch the sunset. I walked through the woods and picked wildflowers. I loved to hear the wind blow through the trees and fill the air with the sent of honeysuckle.

Occasionally little words would spring into my mind; I would put them into verse and go around humming them to myself for days.

When I was about twelve years old, I wrote my first Gospel song. I would sing the lines and verses to myself; I was so shy I would not let anyone know what I was doing. I was afraid they would make fun of me.

At that time, I had only one close friend. We went to school together and we would visit each other on weekends. Usually, I would spend the weekend at her house. The two of us would go down the road to an old barn on their place, so we could feed and milk the cow; that was her chore. She tried to teach me to milk the cow, but with out success. Every time I got close to the cow, it would swipe its tail in my face; the milk bucket would go one way and I would go the other. I never did learn to milk a cow.

My friend and I would practice singing gospel songs together while she did the milking. We learned how to harmonize and we got good at it. I told her about the song I had written and sang it for her. She got all excited. Some of her family members were Pentecostal ministers. They held revivals, brush arbor meetings and all day sings. They would go to different locations around the area and have church and prayer meetings. Most of them could sing and play instruments. My friend told them about my new song, they heard it and liked it and they started taking me to their services and let me sing it to the congregation. They even had a guitar player to back me up. I did not know back then how to put a chorus or bridge into a song. I just wrote verses and sang them straight through. Even so, the people loved my song. They told me that God had given me a gift for writing. I was twelve years old and I guess being a little country kid, I liked the attention.

18

My dad did not believe in the Pentecostal way and when he found out I was going to their meetings, he would only let me attend if a family member went with me. He thought they were devil people and that they were somehow going to cast a spell on me. However, my aunt, my mother's sister, had been attending those services and daddy said I could go as long as she went with me. It would be years before the (*Pentecostal*) spell would claim me. I have always kept the memory of those times in those meetings; singing my little songs for the Lord, it warms my heart and I know that is where God planted a seed in my heart, which would take years to sprout and bloom. Except for a few songs in a few nightclubs, later in my life, singing in the Pentecostal meetings was the extent of my singing. Many years later, I started writing and singing gospel songs in the church where I gave my broken life to Jesus.

Chapter 7

RESCUED

The nineteen-fifties came in with our country still at war, this time with Korea. I was now in my early teens. Many of the young boys in our area had enlisted or drafted into the military. It would be a time of more changes for our country; even the music would change from Pop and Easing Listening, to Rock and Roll, and would teach us new ways of dancing. We would learn the Jitterbug, Twist, and Cha-cha. We now had electricity, and my dad purchased our first black and white television set. We could now watch, American Bandstand, I love Lucy; Leave it to Beaver; Lassie, and The little Rascals. We learned to dance by watching the Bandstand on the television set. My life would begin with a whirlwind of changes also.

Somewhere during the summer of nineteen, fifty-two, I met my first love. We became friends as we worked side by side in the fields. He had left home and taken a job on my uncle's farm. The job paid him little more than room and board. Falling in love was not in our plans. We talked a lot and shared many things because we had the same background, but I could never bring myself to tell him of certain parts of my childhood. He was sixteen and I was fourteen, just two kids who knew nothing of life outside of the hardships in the Mississippi Delta. He became my hero.

In nineteen-fifty-three he enlisted in the military, 82nd Airborne Div. We kept in touch by mail all through his basic training. He was under eighteen years old when he enlisted. During the Korean War, a boy could get into the military at that age with a parent's consent. Back then, we had to communicate by U.S. mail because only the town's people had telephones and the Internet not yet heard of. The country was at war and I was constantly afraid that he was going to ship to Korea any day.

It was also during this time that I got my first job, in a sewing factory. We made jackets and pants for the military. The pay was fifty-two cents an hour. I thought I was rich every time I got my paycheck. Many of us lied about our ages to get the jobs. I was fourteen years old and daddy did not know I had to be sixteen to work in a factory, so he let me work.

My Pentecostal aunt was also working there, so that meant that I had to stay with her and my uncle during the week so I could ride thirty miles to work each day with her and the other girls whom we carpooled. I liked staying with them, but I liked going home on the weekends so I could be with my own family, I missed my mother, little sister and my brothers. I was excited and happy, because I thought my dreams were coming true.

By this time, my boy friend was completing his basic training, and would soon be home on his first leave; I was working my first real job, and felt all grown up. I had kept my job in the factory for a few months, when a big boss from Chicago came down for an inspection and discovered how young many of us girls were and had to lay us off. He told me when I got old enough I could come back to work. Now that I had dreams of getting married, it really did not disappoint me that I was losing my job.

My boy friend returned on his first leave, he purposed to me and I accepted; we became engaged, and I was feeling like Cinderella. I was fifteen at that time; and we were married two months after my sixteenth birthday. For the first time in my life, I was out of the cotton fields, away from all those who had abused me and I was very happy. He was my hero because he had rescued me from all the things I hated and feared. In truth, I took all of the fears, shame, guilt and confusion with me.

It is hard to remember just when it started to go wrong for us. We were now living in a military town, near Fort Bragg, N.C. My husband seldom drank. On the few occasions that he became intoxicated, the demon he kept on leash inside himself broke loose. He would go into such rages that I would be terrified. He never raised a hand to me, but the walls and anything else in his way at the time suffered. In these incidents, my mind would revert to my childhood, and the memories of my dad's drunken violence would come back to haunt me. Times were different back then, and we were both much too young to take on the responsibilities of a marriage. In the end, it would be a disaster.

My husband had buried the cause of his rage, the way I had buried the reasons for my distance. I could not understand why he had so much rage inside or why he would have these fits of anger as his father was a preacher and his mother was one of the Godliest women I ever knew;

he never told me what happened in his past that left him traumatized. He could no more tell me his pain than I could tell him mine. The childhood traumas we had both suffered hung on in the heart and mind of each of us and gradually tore us apart. We separated for the first time before our first anniversary. He did his stint in the military then reenlisted for another term, which meant transferring to a different military base where I would join him for a while. We would try very hard to make our marriage work but it always ended up the same way with separations, reconciliations and more separations. He believed I did not love him and he found comfort elsewhere. Finally, the only answer was divorce. I filed for divorce and then discovered I was now pregnant with my first child; and so the little dream world I had weaved around me was coming unraveled.

On August 6, nineteen-fifty-six, just a few months before our divorce was final, was the birthday of our son, my firstborn. How can I describe this child? He was beautiful from the day he was born. He came into the world pouring out love. He had no way of knowing what cards life would deal him. I had gone back home to Mississippi to have my baby, my husband was still in the military, now stationed at Fort Bliss, Texas. I was eighteen years old, in the middle of a divorce, with an infant son. I had such mixed up ideas and terrible feelings of failure. I had yet to learn what life was all about.

My advice here for young people is to wait until you are old enough and mature enough to know what it means to be married. Enjoy your youth while it is yours, and seek God's wisdom in who you choose for a partner. Marriage should be a lifetime commitment, and will leave scars when broken. It left scars on me that would last for a lifetime.

Chapter 8

THE NIGHTMARES

On September 5, nineteen-fifty-six, my baby barely a month old, I found myself in the middle of a hell. I was now staying at my parent's home, and my dad was still heavy on the booze. My older sister had married and my older brother had just gone to live in Chicago. My younger sister, two little brothers, my mother, my infant son and myself were at home that Saturday night. We lived in an old country house, without a telephone and miles from the nearest neighbor. Daddy was drunk; he was arguing with my mother and I knew he was going to hit her; so, I stepped between them, all ninety-eight pounds of me against a full-grown man in a drunken rage. The first blow caught me on my nose, breaking it in three places.

The beating started in my mother's kitchen and ended up leaving a bloody trail from there to the front driveway. I tried to run but could not get my feet to move. I was pouring blood all over the place and he just kept on beating me. I finally realized that he was going to kill me if I did not get away. I managed to break lose and run for the front porch. I tripped and fell off the porch onto the gravel driveway. He caught me by my hair, dragging me through gravel and broken glass, beating me with his fists until my clothes were soaked in blood. I was sure he was going to take my life. I was strangling on my own blood. I could feel the dark cloud of death all around me. I remember begging him to stop, but my begging was no more than a whimper. I was nearly unconscious, but I knew if I passed out, I would be dead. The fear of death was worse than the beating itself. After all else failed to pull daddy off of me, my sister and younger brothers took off running down the road to the nearest neighbor to get help.

By the time help arrived and I was taken to the hospital, I was almost dead from loss of blood and I was going into shock. My nose was broken, my lips were torn and swollen, one tooth was broken, and much of my hair torn out and my eyes were swollen shut. There were cuts and bruises all over my body. The doctor had to pick rocks and broken glass out of my arms and legs. My face had been so badly beaten it took many weeks for it to heal. I was a mess! I remember it like yesterday!

23

For a long time after enduring that beating, I would wake up in the middle of the night with the feeling that I was suffocating. I was trying to spit blood out of my mouth and I could feel the same blackness closing in on me that I had felt that night. I would wake up in a cold sweat, trembling in the darkness. Sometimes I would have dreams of running into the woods, fleeing the boogieman. Just before he would catch me, I would wake up, terrified.

The nightmares would fade away for a while, only to come back every time I encountered violence of any kind. I had always been afraid of guns, knives or any kind of weapon, although the only weapon used that night was my daddy's fist. To me they were just as deadly as the others were. Until that awful night, daddy had only raised a hand, physically, to me once in my life when I was a little girl. However, that night he was a drunken monster and my only thought was to protect my mother from his wrath. The beating I endured was worth it for her.

My face and body healed slowly, leaving only a tiny scar on my nose, but the scars left on my heart and soul stayed there for many years. After that episode, in addition to the fears and feelings of inferiority that plagued me, I was full of anger and hatred toward my father. It ate at me like a cancer. I did not suspect how those feelings would shape my life. It would be a long time and a lot of heartache later, before I would learn to forgive and find healing.

My father had a stroke in nineteen sixty-seven. It disabled him and took much of his memory. He forgot about the pain he had caused his family, and I never mentioned the past. By this time, I had given my life to Jesus; was active in my church and trying to be a good example for my children. Daddy would come to visit, listen to gospel music and tell me how proud he was of me. I praised God for the change in him, whatever the reason. My dad passed away in nineteen seventy-three. I believe he made peace with God before he died. For that, I am grateful and am always amazed at the mercies of God.

Chapter 9

DRIFTING

The latter part of the fifties, in a way, was a year of drifting. I spent a few months in Mississippi, a few months in New Orleans, a few months in Oklahoma with my former in-laws, who were still very dear friends to me. They were wonderful people and ministers of the gospel; at that time, they were pastors in a Church of God there. They continued to love me and prayed that their son and I would somehow reconcile. However, that would not happen. I have always thanked God for putting these people in my life. At that time, I was so lost and I was completely unaware of what my problem was. However, they knew and in their love for God and their love for me, they never gave up in their prayers for my salvation.

To me the worst part of being lost was the loneliness; that feeling inside that you cannot quite fill, no matter what you do. Each day brought a different set of emotions. One day I would feel hate and bitterness; the next day I would feel an overwhelming love, with no one to share that love. I decided feeling hatred hurt less. I learned at an early age how to hide my feelings, how to pretend that things were just fine, when in reality, nothing was just fine at all.

No one knew the secrets I carried around inside me, the feelings of fear, pain and inferiority. I thought I was not as good as other people. I did not know then that what I needed to fill the hole in me was a relationship with Jesus. I continued to make one mistake after another; riding the roller coaster that was my life, moving too swiftly to see anything and going too fast to stop.

I finally moved to Chicago to live with my older brother and his new wife. I got a job and was able to support my two-year-old little boy and myself. With the help of my brother and the friendship of my new sister-in-law, I was beginning to get my life back together, or so I thought.

Most of the abuse I suffered up until that time came from alcohol. Therefore, I never thought I would ever fall into that pit. However, Satan wants to damn every soul he can. His strongest weapons are deception and addictions. If he can deceive us into feeling guilty, afraid, and ashamed or unworthy, he can cause us to try to escape those feelings by indulging in substance or behaviors that lead to addictions. I had a front row seat in his classroom and I was an excellent student.

Chapter 10

THE LONG ROAD

Reading this chapter will leave some to believe that I was not thinking clearly during the years depicted. I was at a place in my life where I was coasting, unable or unready to face my problems and deal with them. I started dating; I was young, pretty, and tired of being lonely. Being a divorcee back then, was an entirely different type of label, than it is today. I learned, early in this episode of my life, that most men looked at a divorced woman differently than they looked at single women. I was not willing to play their games. After going through the propositions and rejections, I convinced myself that all men were the same. They only wanted to use me for their own selfish reasons. I was eager to remarry and make a home for my child and a husband. I was ready to be happy and share my life with someone who would care for me. I vowed that if I should find that someone, I would stay married for the rest of my life. I would not fail again. I would never be a divorcee again.

In nineteen fifty-nine, while still living in Chicago, I met my second husband. He was good looking and charming. We were married three weeks after we met. If we had given ourselves sufficient time to get to know each other, I do not think we would have married at all, at least not at that time. On the day we married, however, I pledged to myself that I would stay married this time, no matter what I had to do to make the marriage work. Were we in love? How can you be in love with someone you hardly know? I was vulnerable and scared in those days. He said, let us get married, I said, sure, why not? The answer to my question came much too quickly. My new husband was a rambler and a gambler. He played the bars and clubs from Chicago's North side to the South side and all in between. He left me one week after our wedding without warning or explanation. I was stunned and hurt. I realized I had made a terrible mistake; one that I had promised not to correct. With no more warning than his leaving, he reappeared two weeks later. He had just been out of town with some friends on a gambling spree, was his explanation.

We lived in Chicago for almost a year after we were married. We then decided to move to Memphis, Tennessee. My little boy, now three years old, was growing fast. He was the most important reason to try to make my new marriage work; hoping my husband would settle down and make a home. We had been in Memphis for a few months; I had a job and I was glad for the work. My husband became dissatisfied again and decided that Houston, Texas was the place to be. He left once more, sending for the two of us after several weeks. The time we spent together in Houston came to an abrupt end after only three weeks.

I had to separate from my husband for the same reasons that we had parted previously, drinking, gambling and all the other things that are part of that lifestyle. I remember him coming home that afternoon, drunk and belligerent, we had a fight and he passed out. I took my son, caught a bus and went back to Memphis. My husband was waiting for me when the bus pulled into the Memphis station. Because of my bus stops, he was able to beat me back to Memphis. It was to be one of many such episodes, as we would make our way through our life together.

For a short period, we both seemed to be making an effort to make a better life. Then, unexpectedly, he wanted to go back to Chicago. Jobs were better there he argued. At least this time when we uprooted and moved, we did it together. We were young, he was restless and we were both lost. I got my old job back and we settled into the same routine. This pattern would repeat itself repeatedly.

If I might pause here and clarify the fact that I do not place all the blame on my husband for the hardships we brought on ourselves. I was just as lost as he was and we were just doing what sinners do. I am sure there were things I could have done better had I known how to do them. Nevertheless, sinners do not stop sinning until they come to the only one who can change them, and that is Jesus Christ and he alone.

Chapter 11

A Decade of Turmoil

The nineteen sixties would bring in another decade of turmoil for our country, with the Vietnam War speeding up that would last into the next decade. We also had the Civil Rights Movement, Integration, Boycotts and School bombings. It would also be a time of mourning for our country, with the assassination of our President in 1963, the assassination of a United States Senator followed by the assassination of a well-known Civil Rights Leader in 1968.

For us it would be the beginning of our family together. In this decade, we would bring into the world, five of our six children together, three boys and one girl, with another girl later on, to join my son from my previous marriage, and give us a family of seven children, whom we both adored.

Our first child together, a boy, was born December 18, nineteen-sixty. My husband arrived at the hospital just minutes before I went into delivery. I had not seen him in two weeks and it would be three weeks before I would see him again. I left the hospital fourteen hours after I had arrived and went back to work nine days later.

Chicago is a very cold place in January. I remember standing in the snow, waiting for a bus to take me to work every morning in sub-zero temperatures. I had returned to the same job and my boss gave me light work as he could see I was weak and still recovering from childbirth.

My husband continued to work the bars. He was everything from bouncer to bartender. If I wanted to see him, I knew where to find him. I began to think if I went out with him more often, maybe I could get him to come home at a decent hour. However, all I accomplished was to create two bar flies where there had been only one.

Until that time, I had tasted liquor three times in my life and did not like it, so I never drank it. Although my husband worked in bars, I was not accustomed to the bar scene. Nevertheless, as all things must start somewhere and as in most cases, those things start in little increments, 10 pm one night, 12 pm the next night. One drink, two drinks, three drinks, more drinks until you forget that your intentions were good and you have become a big part of the problem. We would party every weekend and sometimes in between. It did not take me long, however, to tire of being in the bars and I did not like leaving my little boys with sitters so often. By this time, I liked the effects of the liquor; it numbed the pain and helped me through the guilt. The solution was easy; I would just drink at home.

I then became a solitary drinker. I would work my shift and stop at the liquor store on the way home. I would feed my boys, put them to bed and drink myself to sleep, go to work the next morning and repeat the same actions repeatedly. My husband was not home long enough to notice what was happening to me. Would he have cared if he had known? I do not think so, as long as it did not inconvenience him. We were both guilty of the same sin, rejecting Jesus.

Was I an alcoholic? I think I was in danger of becoming one, but I never got to the place to where I could not live without another drink, however, that was by the Grace of God. I never smoked pot nor did any kind of drugs, but I think had drugs been so readily available and as rampant as today, I might have tried them too. I was in the throws of a common addiction of the time; however, I smoked two or more packs of cigarettes a day. I was battling flashbacks from my childhood, fighting a loneliness I could not escape, smoking like a chimney and now I had a drinking problem. My life was a bigger mess than ever. On top of all of this, I learned I was pregnant with my third child.

My husband had been gone for more than a month and returned one day after I gave birth to my third son, as usual, without excuse or explanation. I had worked until my due date and returned to the job three weeks after the birth. The same old dance began once more. I began drinking again. I would sit at the bar where my husband was working and wait for his shift to end. Occasionally we would go to other places together after he was off, but most often I was sent home in a cab so he could go out with his friends to party and gamble until the wee hours of the morning. Sometimes he came home and sometimes he did not. I would drink myself to sleep.

I continued in this self-destructive behavior until one morning I awoke with a feeling of disgust for what I had become. I had to clean myself up for my boys. I would walk the streets of Chicago late in the night turning it all over in my mind, trying to figure out what I needed to do. I would remember my childhood and relive all the mistakes I had made trying to create a better life for myself. The memories of the assaults I had endured as a child would rise up in me and I would blame all of my failures on the boogiemen.

The little songs I had written as a child ran through my mind and my tears would flow. I was aware that whatever changes I needed to make, I did not have the strength to make alone. I was so lost, so lonely, so afraid and so full of feelings of self-loathing and despair. I thought of suicide, but in the end, I knew I could not leave my babies unprotected in a cruel world.

I found not only was I unable to make any changes, but I feared to make them. At least I knew what to expect now. My husband continued to party, I continued to drink and things continued to get worse. I began to realize that my husband's gambling had escalated. He had a serious problem. He would be gone most of the time, returning home only long enough to take a nap, shower, change clothes and leave again. Sometimes he would not come home for days. As time wore on his absences would last for months. I would then be alone to support and raise my children.

I considered the idea of divorce, as much as I hated to break my pledge, but fear ruled my mind. I had learned from experience that my husband was a very violent man. He had threatened me more than once and I was afraid to leave him for fear of what he might do. I remembered the beating I had taken at the hands of my father. I was so cowed and afraid I abandoned the idea of a divorce.

I worked everyday and took care of my boys, but my drinking continued. I realized I was almost at the end of my rope when it got harder for me to drink and continue to function. I had nowhere else to turn, so I turned to prayer. I did not know my prayers did not go anywhere, as I was not praying in repentance or for the Glory of God. I was just grasping for straws. I attended church occasionally, but that only made me feel guiltier. I stopped going.

We moved several times in a rapid succession, Illinois, Ohio, Mississippi, Tennessee, Texas, and Alabama. We ended up in Birmingham, finally. We found jobs, bought a house and I hoped we would never move again. It did not take long, however, for the allure of the bar scene to attract my husband. The new leaf that we had turned over was in reality a leaf on the same old book. All the old behaviors returned, to both of us. The drinking and partying became just as big a part of this new life as it had been in the old; the only difference was that I did not drink as much or as often as I had before.

31

By the spring of nineteen sixty-four, we were back in Chicago. Our type of move was not as expensive as one might think. Gas was around thirty cents a gallon and we moved only what we could fit into the vehicle we had at the time. Usually we rented a furnished apartment. Sometimes we were able to find a furnished house we could afford. We would start all over again. I lost count of how many times we started over.

My husband returned to the same old bars, I returned to the same old job, and our lives continued in the same old way for another year, and then, I became pregnant again and things were not looking good. I took my little boys, left my husband and went back to my family in Mississippi. My husband chose to remain in Chicago. Because I had neither money nor insurance, I was unable to see a doctor until a few weeks before my child's birth. I delivered my forth son on April 14, nineteen-sixty-five. One month later, the boys and I rode a train back to Chicago, and to my husband. Life went on once again.

By this time, my husband had secured a real job, as a painter. He worked in the high-rise buildings sprouting all over the city. His day job did not hamper his nighttime activities. He was drinking, partying and gambling as he always did. I did not return to work and I did not go back to the bars. My oldest son was in school and I knew that somehow, someway we had to settle down and raise our children. I had no idea how to get my husband to accept these facts. I was twenty-six years old with four little boys to care for and my roller coaster life was moving so fast it kept my head spinning.

Chapter 12

CONVICTION AND CONVERSION

I made up my mind to get my children and myself out of Chicago, no matter what it took. One night, as I walked from bar to bar, looking for my husband I talked to God, or at least, I talked at God. I promised him that I would do anything for him, if he would get us away from this place. I walked back to our apartment and forgot about it. Strange as it may seem, one week later, my husband decided we should move back to my hometown in Mississippi. For me it would be the best move we ever made.

Just a few weeks after we moved back to Mississippi, I met two young Christian women, at the place where we worked. They were married to two brothers who were both ministers and they became my friends. When they invited me to go to their church where their husbands were holding a revival, I accepted.

The first time I attended service proved the best day of my life. God touched my heart and forgave my sins and for the first time in my life, I felt clean and free. God put me in the right place at the right time and sent the right women to witness to me and I have never been the same since that night. I can remember it like yesterday. It was on a Sunday night about 8pm, December 14, nineteen-sixty-five when I accepted Jesus as my Savior and all that pain and shame and guilt just washed away. Praise God!

There had been no church nearby to attend when I was growing up, so I did not have any religious training of any kind. My mother must have known God because I would hear her praying to him frequently. At some point, when I was still a child, a Baptist preacher came to our area, erected a tent, and started a revival. Daddy took all of us children to the meetings. At the end of the revival, he took us into town to a Baptist church and had us baptized. Not one of us knew what baptism meant. That was the only time I remember ever being inside a church in my childhood.

I did not know that a person must acknowledge that he/she is a sinner, and repent of that sin. As a child, I equated sinners with the bad men who hurt and molested me. I did not understand that everyone is a sinner, and that each of us must repent of our sin in order to receive the gift of salvation. The only gospel I had heard back then was at the meetings of the Pentecostal believers who allowed me to sing my song for them. Those good people believed that God had bestowed this talent upon me. I did not know anything about a gift from God, but I did know there was a God. I now know that he had been calling me all through those troubled years, but I failed to recognize his voice because I was not listening to his knock on my hearts door until the tapping kept getting louder. I began trying to change my ways. I tried to quit all my bad habits. I gave up the drinking, and tried to keep the anger down so I would not cuss as much. I stopped going with my husband to the bars. I started reading books on the Bible and began to think I was doing okay.

The term conviction means to be aware of your sins. The term, conversion means to turn around and go in the opposite direction. It did not take God a long time to save me; it just took me a long time to convert. While I was reading my Bible and books about the Bible, saying lay-me-down-to-sleep prayers, trying to clean myself up so I would be good enough to come to God, I was just wasting my time and his!

Only when I realized I was helpless to save myself and that nothing I could do would make me worthy of his love, could he save me. When I looked inside myself and saw my sins, I saw only myself, not the people and events I had blamed all of my life; it was just Jesus and me. It was my sins I had to confess, not the sins of my father or the boogiemen, and not the sins of my husband. It was as if my whole life passed before me and all I had to do was give it to God and as I did that, I knew I would never be the same. I had just stepped from darkness into his marvelous light and that light has been guiding me ever since.

Chapter 13

BORN AGAIN

(The baptism in the Holy Ghost, what does it mean)
(All Bible quotations taken from King James Version of the Bible)

I am a simple person, lacking the skills necessary to explain the new birth, and the Baptism of the Holy Ghost. I can only go by God's word and my own experience. The term born again is misused now days. Even the politicians are using it as a tool to get more votes. Jesus said you should know them by the fruits they bare.

(John 3:1-3) There was a man of the Pharisees, named Nicodemus, a ruler of the Jews. The same came to Jesus by night and said unto Him, Rabbi, we know that thou art a teacher, sent from God, for no man can do these miracles that thou doest, except God be with him. Jesus answered and said unto him, Verily, verily, I say unto you, except a man be born again, he cannot see the kingdom of God.

(John 4:14.) Whosoever drinketh of the water that I shall give him shall never thirst; but the water that I shall give him shall be in him a well of water springing up into everlasting life.

(John 8:38) If the Son therefore, shall make you free, ye shall be free indeed.

(John 6:44) No man can come to me, except the Father who hath sent me, draw him; and I will raise him up the last day.

(John 15:16) Ye have not chosen me, but I have chosen you, that ye should go and bring forth fruit and that your fruit should remain; that whatsoever ye shall ask of my Father in my name, he may give you.

So many people think that good works and good behavior will ensure their admittance into Heaven. They are so tragically wrong. Only when they have accepted Jesus Christ as their Lord and Savior can they know salvation. There is a Heaven, there is a Hell, and eventually, we are going to one of them. It is up to each of us to choose which one.

We do not just wake up one morning and say to ourselves, I am going to change my ways and start living right. Stopping bad habits, putting on more clothes or cleaning up our languages, will not save us. We are not saved by joining a church, singing in the choir, paying our tithes or doing well to our neighbor; nor are we saved by being baptized in water and we do not grow into salvation. We grow in grace and knowledge of the Lord after reading God's word and applying it to our lives. We are helpless to save ourselves from sin that we inherited from Adam, who brought the curse of sin to all humanity. It matters not what lifestyle we come from; if we are rich or poor; if every person in our background was a Christian; or if we belong to the most prestigious church in town. We are born again when we confess with our mouths the Lord Jesus and believe in our heart that God raised him from the dead. It is when we accept him into our heart and make him Lord of our lives that we are born again. It is then that he will cast our sins into the sea of forgetfulness and remember them against us no more. (Eph. 2:8) *For by grace ye are saved, through faith; and that not of yourselves: it is the gift of God: not of works, lest any man should boast.*

God dealt with me for a long time before he saved me, because I was trying to find him. The phrase, I found the Lord, some use to explain their salvation, is incorrect because he was never lost. He had been calling me and I would not hear. He called me when I was a little girl, when he was my imaginary friend. He called me every time I heard his word. He called me every time someone prayed for me. He called me many times through my troubles. He called me when I was near death, but he did not choose me until I opened my heart and let him in.

I always had a Bible and now and then when I would get desperate; I would pull it out and read a verse or two of scripture that fit my needs, as many people will do. Then I would try to draw some kind of strength from it, but I did not know how to commit myself to what it was saying to me. Until I confessed my sins and accepted God's forgiveness there was no way to finding the peace I needed. Only then, did he save me and change me. I was no longer the same person I had been. (Second Corinthians, 5:17) Therefore, if any man is in Christ Jesus, he is a new creature; old things have passed away; behold all things become new.

I did not feel any of the sweeping emotions some experience when they are born again. What I felt was a peace I had never known; and an excitement that I did not understand. I knew with certainty, that I was free from my sins, and the guilt and shame I had carried all of my life. The first change I noticed in myself occurred the next morning. The cussing and cursing were gone from my mouth. I felt as if I had truly been reborn as a new person. He gave me joy to replace my sadness; he put a song in my heart that continues its melody to this day. He justified me and remade me as if I had never sinned.

When God saved me, I had to forgive all the ones who had hurt me or I could not find forgiveness for my own sins. It takes God's forgiveness to save our soul, but it takes our forgiveness toward others to heal our broken heart. God's promise is that the blood of Jesus Christ will cleanse us from all sin. That means the sins we have committed and the sins that others have committed against us. He taught me how that forgiving others would bring healing to my own heart.

From that day, Jesus was my Savior, my Lord and my best friend. I accepted baptism in water and received the Baptism in the Holy Ghost shortly thereafter. (Baptism of the Holy Ghost is in the book of Acts.) Baptism in water is a public profession of faith that we have been born again. Our emersion under the water signifies the death and burial, of our old man of sin. Then we rise from the water to a new life in Christ. We must be born again by the Spirit of God.

Baptism in the Holy Ghost came on the day of Pentecost and is the infilling of God's Spirit that empowers the believer to be a witness to the greatness of God. One of the manifestations of the Holy Ghost is the gift of tongues. Although the gift of tongues is only one of the gifts, it is the power of God in us to work his will. When we walk in the Spirit, we have perfect communion with God.

(Acts 2: 16-18) This is that spoken by the prophet Joel; *and it shall come to pass in the last days, saith God; I will pour out of my Spirit upon all flesh: and your sons and your daughters shall prophesy, and your young men shall see visions, and your old men shall dream dreams. And on my servants and on my handmaidens I will pour out in those days of my Spirit; and they shall prophesy.*

(Mark 16:17) *And these signs will follow those who believe: In my name they will cast out demons; they will speak with new tongues."*

I started studying the Bible and it just came alive for me, I could hardly put it down. I followed his story from the manger to the cross; learned all of his teachings, read about the miracles and wonders he did; how he was sinless and innocent in all his ways, yet they found him guilty. How could I not fall in love with Jesus Christ? I was sorry that I had waited so long to learn what he could do and how happy I could be in him. I am amazed at how foolish people really are; they found him guilty of what crime, love in the first degree? I cannot comprehend how much suffering Jesus endured for our salvation and to realize it was for me also, and had I been the only person in the world, he would have done it all just for me.

I can better explain the works of the Holy Ghost in my own simple terminology. When I sat by the bedside of my dying son, he sat with me! When my child was in despair, he touched her! When I had no food or shelter for my children, he supplied the need! When I was on my deathbed, he healed me! When I walked the last mile I could walk; he picked me up and carried me! When I was tempted, he delivered me! When I could not find words sufficient to praise Him, he gave me tongues of fire! The unknown tongues is the gift of the Holy Ghost to enable a believer to communicate directly with God and when we pray in tongues, the Spirit is interceding for us in a language that no one else can understand and the devil cannot intercept. This gift is for all believers who will ask and receive it. He has been my father, counselor, comforter, healer and my best friend. He is worthy of praise.

God never does anything by accident and he is never surprised. He has reasons for placing situations, events and people in our lives; sometimes these things are hard and hurtful, but he knows best what it takes to get our attention and draw us to him. In my case, he used a group of Pentecostal believers when I was twelve years old, later in my life, he sent other Christian people to love and pray for me. Through the prayers and witness of God's people, his Holy Spirit drew me to him, which is why I am a witness for him today.

Did my salvation make me perfect? No! Did it take away all my problems? No! What it did was give me strength beyond myself to deal with the cares of life and it put a joy in my heart that kept me singing all day long. I sang when I did my house work; I sang to my kids and when I was on the job, I sang to myself. I was not a happy person, but I was joyful. From that time on, I never found the need for any counselor other than my pastor and Jesus. From that time on until very late in life, I was never sick. God's power kept me on my feet and gave me strength to care for my loved ones and to continue doing what I could to glorify his name.

Did he step down to earth and talk to me personally? The Bible says, in the beginning was the Word, and the Word was God. Therefore, when I read his word, to me it is the same as hearing his voice speak to me, even though I cannot see him, I can feel his presence. Every time we hear his word; every time someone prays for us; every time we read a Bible verse, even if it is on a sign by the side of a road, it is God calling us. No matter if, God's word comes forth from the mouth of an infidel, it is still his word, and it is up to us to stop, hear his voice and really listen to what he is saying to us. He is asking us to see the greatest gift known to man.

(Hebrews 4:12) The word of God is quick, and powerful, and sharper than any two-edged sword, piercing even to the dividing asunder of soul and spirit, and of the joints and marrow, and is a discerner of the thoughts and intents of the heart.

I had stopped writing songs or anything else, for some time. After my conversion, I joined the church and starting writing again. Now the words were just bubbling out of my heart. God put the words there and I pinned them down and sang them every chance that I got. I always knew when one of my songs touched the church members by their response. When I sang I could feel God flowing through me and the realities of my life seemed far away.

The first time I sang my song at a church service; many of the people came to tell me that God had given me a gift for writing. I still did not know why God would give someone like me a special gift. I was very shy about singing my songs to a building full of people, but every time I wrote a new song, I would sing it in the church and God blessed me in everything I wrote.

I attended the Church of God in Clarksdale, Mississippi from nineteen sixty-five through nineteen eighty-seven. When I joined the church, my oldest son was eight years old and my three younger sons were from eight months to five years old; my youngest three were born in the next seven years and the children and I spent most of their growing up years in the same church. Going to worship service, Sunday school, Bible studies, homecomings and youth camps were a way of life for us. I hold those memories close to my heart, for it was there that God saved me and grounded me in my faith as I learned through his word and my own experiences, that God is always the God of today and he is not bound by man's traditions and he does not live in man's time zone.

Chapter 14

DOWN FROM THE MOUNTAINS

My husband was staying away from home for longer periods at this point. Sometimes I knew where he was, but most often, I did not know. I would put my children to bed at night and I would write my hurt and loneliness and my faith into songs. It got to the place in our lives where I was glad when my husband did not come home. At least when he was not there, I had no one to curse and scream at me. I could put my kids to bed knowing another late-night fight would not awaken them.

After my spiritual experiences, I was on a glorious high. Being a Christian was the most exciting thing that had ever happened in my life. I was on top of the world. I had a joy and a peace in my heart that surpasses all understanding. The spiritual mountaintop that I had reached was not to be my resting place however. God meant for me to learn and grow and to do that, I had to leave the mountaintop behind and trudge through the deeper valleys of life. I was to learn, my painful journey through those valleys had only begun.

Although changes happened to me, the harshness of my life did not change. My husband would stay away for months at a time, leaving me to find a job, to feed and house my children. I worked in factories, restaurants, country stores and then I would sew for friends, relatives and church members at night to earn extra money. My church and my Christian friends would help me through many of these times. From them I learned about faith and love.

I recall one of the times when I thought I was not going to survive the hardships I was facing. My husband had left me with four little boys, the youngest being eighteen months old and I was pregnant with my fifth child. The old house we lived in was cold, drafty in the winter, hot, and miserable in the summer. The winter was worse because I could not afford the butane gas to heat the whole house. I put my children all together on a mattress in the warmest room and covered them with all the blankets I could find. Because I had no transportation I had to ride thirty-five miles to work, five days a week with a co-worker, it was necessary for my children to be up and ready for the school bus or sitter by daylight. Sometimes, no matter what I did, there was not enough food to last from one payday to the next; neither welfare nor food stamps back then to fall back on. Sometimes a friend would bring food and say, the Lord told me you needed this.

There was no money for doctors, no insurance either. If one of the children got sick, I would call the church and we would pray. I learned what faith in God could do. I saw God's miracles work in our lives repeatedly. On April 26, nineteen sixty-seven, God sent our first daughter. I had been sick with worry as how I was going to take care of another child, almost without funds and no husband in sight. I had worked in a factory as long as I could work, until three weeks before my baby's due date. Then I had to move in with relatives until my baby was born. I sewed and did anything I could do to contribute to our room and board. I cried and prayed to God that, I just cannot do this anymore; I was at the end of my rope. I know now that the birth of all my children and the raising them, mostly alone, was the tempering of my faith. God gave me seven children to give my life purpose and to strengthen me: He created my children to fulfill the purposes of his Devine will for them and for me.

My husband had been gone since very early in my pregnancy. I had delivered our beautiful daughter, gone back to work, rented a house, filed for divorce and was on my way to starting over, once again; without a clue as to how I was going to accomplish that and then, he reappeared; same old tears, same old promises. He had secured a good job in Memphis, he said and everything would be different, would be better, if the children and I would go back with him. I had heard all of this before, but the look on the faces of my children and my belief that they needed their father, held sway once again. I still held strong convictions on marriage and divorce and knew I must follow God's will, no matter what it cost. The divorce canceled, our belongings packed, we were off to Memphis once again.

41

Chapter 15

UPRISING IN MEMPHIS

B y the summer of that year, we had settled in and life continued its steady pace forward. Two boys were in school, two more were playing at my feet and our baby girl was growing fast. With five children to care for it was impossible for me to go back to work and I was glad to be home with my brood. I found a new church and enrolled my children in Sunday school and life seemed to be going in the right direction this time. My husband's steady income made things a bit easier and I had more confidence in the future than ever before. We had a real Christmas that year and the coming New Year promised to be even better.

Snow fell early in April, nineteen sixty-eight, a very unusual event for Memphis, Tennessee, but there was little beauty in it. The garbage-strewn streets turned the pristine white snow to muck as soon as it fell. The garbage worker's strike had been going on for some weeks and the city was becoming a garbage dump. A well-known Civil Rights Leader had come to the city to mediate an agreement between the City of Memphis and the garbage workers; he became assassinated at a hotel just a few blocks from where we lived. The city erupted into violence; people rioting in the garbage-laden streets; snipers shooting at random; buildings engulfed in flames, the work of arsonists; looting of all businesses; attacks on law enforcement personal and firefighters; the chaos spread across our country.

My husband and I took the children to my family one hundred miles away, to wait out the danger. We returned after several days, when the National Guard had been able to subdue the rioters. Memphis looked like a war zone; you could actually feel the tension in the air. We felt it was unsafe for the children and decided not to stay. We moved our things back to my hometown in Mississippi.

The return to familiar ground seemed good for all of us. The children and I resumed our attendance at the old church and the boys went back to their old school. Things were good for a while, but my husband's old demons would not be quiet for long. There was only two or three small bar rooms in town, so my husband found the one he liked and took up part time residence. The only good thing about this turn of events is he did come home at night.

On March 23, nineteen sixty-nine, my husband and I welcomed another son into our family and on May 21, nineteen seventy-two, we had another beautiful little girl. My husband had been with me through both pregnancies. However, it seemed the more children we had, the worse the abuse.

During the quite times of my husband's absences, I would reflect on our family life. In times when my husband was at home with us, we did have segments of a normal life, I would draw strength form those times. There had been times spent together; picnicking, camping on the sand bars of the Mississippi river and watching the barges ply the dark water, fishing; watching TV with the kids, making home made ice cream with a crank type ice cream maker and all of us playing ball together. I did not believe my husband was a bad or evil man. I believed he was just a lost soul. I prayed for his deliverance and the peace it would bring to himself and his family.

As the drinking continued to worsen, my husband's actions became erratic and sometimes dangerous. He owned several guns of all types. This was quite normal in our part of the country as most of the men engaged in hunting one thing or another. When my sons were old enough, my husband taught them how to shoot and how to handle a gun. However, on the weekends, when he was drunk and out of control, I would hide the guns; not from him alone, but from our sons, I feared what might happen if he tried to assault them in a drunkard rage. We continued to stay together, or I should say, the children and I stayed put and my husband went where he chose, when he chose and came home if he chose. At times, the violence in our home would send my kids and me to friends or family for refuge. There were many times when I had to call the police for help.

Over the years, I had received much advice from many people, concerning my determination to stay in my marriage. Some of them agreed it was misplaced determination, some said it was lunacy and I should take the children and leave. Maybe some of them were right to say I was too weak or too worn down to leave him. The constant struggle to keep a roof over my children, feed and clothe them, be an example for them and try to avoid the physical and emotional abuse inflected on me, had made it easier to give in; made me afraid to stand my ground.

I would listen to all the advice, but in the end, I was sure it was my duty as a wife and a Christian, to aid in my husband's salvation. The decision to try to save my husband from hell, created a hell on earth for my kids and me. My children heard all the false accusations heaped on me; some of them witnessed a knife thrown, hitting the wall just inches from my head. I was once; whipped with a belt until my body was black and blue. Was all of this God's will? It was not!

Chapter 16

TRYING TO RECOVER

After years of severe alcoholism, my husband decided he had to quit drinking. He tried as hard as he could to stop, but by this time, he could not just quit. The drinking was part of him now, mind and body. Its hold on him would not be broken quickly. Alcohol and/or drugs seeps into a persons mind and changes that person from a decent human being into a fool, and the ones around them have to suffer for their actions. It is not an easy thing to understand, however, it is not a sickness as some claim. It is Sin. If a person drives drunk and kills somebody while under the influence of alcohol or drugs, that person goes to jail and rightfully so. However, no one closes down the liquor stores and bars because the more liquor sold, the more money comes in to fill the pockets of the politicians and keep the lawyers, judges and courts working.

My husband's first arrest for drunk and disorderly would have him ordered into a rehabilitation facility. This was to be one of many such episodes. Being in such a place frightened him. He called our pastor to visit him. They prayed together asking God to forgive my husband's sins and bring him into salvation. Upon his release from the treatment center, he began going to church with his family. I was sure this was the turning point in our lives. Just when we all started to relax and believe in the change in my husband's life, he came home drunk and reverted back to the same old hell.

My friends and family members thought my husband had backslid. I did not agree with that. Once a person has felt the Spirit of God in their souls, there is no going back. What is there in the past that is better than the feeling of peace and security that faith in God imparts? I believe he did not understand the difference between getting sober and salvation, when his demons attacked and tempted him to drink, he did not have the shield of faith to ward off the desire for alcohol.

His drinking continued, but now he drank almost exclusively at home, getting violent, being arrested and admitted to yet another rehab. He would end up admitted to every rehabilitation facility in the state, at least once. The doctors in these treatment centers would detoxify my husband and put him on one kind of prescription medication or another to help him through the physical and emotional trauma of alcohol withdrawal. Years of this kind of treatment created a man with two addictions; alcohol and prescription drugs. I am not a fan of the twenty-eight day wonder type of substance abuse treatment. Statistics prove that they do not work. What works, in my option, is the redeeming grace of God. I know we need doctors and psychiatrists, I believe they are instruments of Devine healing.

I believe that God works his healing miracles in the way he chooses, through the hand of a physician or the counseling of the psychiatrist or by miraculous intervention. In this world, addicts are tagged addicts for their entire lives. That is not right. Jesus said, if the Son hath made you free, you should be free indeed. His promise encompasses all types of addicts.

In the years that followed his first admittance, my husband started his own commercial contracting business. He was very successful and made lots of money. The problem was he spent lots of money. His drinking continued; he sometimes drove two hundred miles to a job, drinking from a bottle of liquor all the way. I prayed every day that God would protect him and not let him get hurt or kill someone on the roads.

By this time, some of my kids were experimenting with drugs and alcohol, dropping out of school; arrested for drunk driving and foolishness. My husband spent a lot of money trying to keep our boys out of trouble, but I believe that only made things worse. They were emulating what they had seen all of their lives. It was to cost them even more dearly than their father. The road they had chosen would be long and hard.

This would put us in the year of nineteen, eighty-six. By this time, my five older children were grown. My oldest son, by my previous marriage, could not take the pressure at home any longer and a few months before his eighteenth birthday, he left home at the age of seventeen to start a new life in Texas. The next two boys had enlisted in the military, another son had moved to Texas. Three of these, my children, would marry and divorce.

If I could single out the worst year in my life, it would be nineteen, eighty-seven. My son-in law, would be electrocuted while turning off the outside lights of the business he managed, during a rainstorm. He barely survived.

One of our younger sons hit a bad spot in the road while riding his motorcycle and the accident put him in the hospital with head injuries, but God was merciful and he pulled through. In September of the same year, my oldest son contracted the AIDS virus; and in December, my youngest son was involved in an automobile accident and almost killed. I mentioned this was the worst year of my life because my husband, as usual, stayed intoxicated. I do not know how much of this he was aware. I felt as though I was drowning in this terror alone. Most of the time I could not answer the phone for fears there would be another tragedy to face and maybe this time it would be worse.

I had no idea that life for me could and would get worse as I kept climbing the mountain ahead of me. I knew that I was either doing something wrong in my life and God was chastising me, or I was doing something right, and the devil was mad at me. I would search my soul repeatedly, trying to find the answers I needed to keep me going. In the end, I knew it was not about right or wrong but God's way of teaching me that I had to trust in him and lean not to my own understanding. Each trial was a stepping-stone to a deeper faith in him and it would take all the faith he could give me for what was still ahead as I kept climbing.

Chapter 17

AIDS
(Acquired Immune Deficiency Syndrome)

In June of nineteen-eighty-eight, we packed up and moved to Dallas, Texas to be close to my son. By this time, the Aids virus was active and my son was very ill. This beautiful, sensitive, intelligent and giving young man was dying with Aids at the age of 32, and turned my already troubled life upside down. He had committed his life to God at the age of fourteen. He had been active in all the youth groups. At sixteen, he was youth director and helped to guide and instruct other young people in our church. At seventeen, he left home; ran from the chaos, rage and hurt and left it behind him. Unfortunately, when he left home, he left God behind also. He got into show business and traveled all over the world. He ran from pain, ran from God, but thankfully, God was waiting for him to slow down.

We moved to Arlington, Texas and lived there for a year. We found jobs and settled in. The Aids virus was taking over my son's body, but not his mind and heart. He was still on his feet, doing everything, he could to help those suffering from the disease and trying to adjust to what was assuredly in his own future.

Soon after we moved to Arlington, scientists were testing a new drug (AZT) that was supposed to send the virus in remission. My son was one of forty-six people in the world who volunteered for the field trials. After almost a year on the new drug, my boy seemed to be doing much better. We were all sure he would survive this terrible disease. I began to go with him to visit Aids patients in the hospital. I had the honor of being able to witness to this marvelous group of people. I learned the real meaning of God's love. There were no barriers in this place, no skin colors, no ethnic differences and no political opinions, only people hoping to live or at worst, hoping to die, peacefully. Each of them needed to feel loved; each of them showed gratitude for any act of kindness; a hug or just a handshake. I was amazed at the love they had for each other.

I also learned of the misinformation that afflicted people's minds and hearts. The disease could spread in few ways, affecting all sexes, age groups, but not in the ridiculous ways people believed. Even ministers in different churches declared that this illness was a punishment on people of certain groups, for a certain type of sin. Regardless of how an individual contracted this deadly sickness, each one of them was entitled to compassion and understanding. They did not deserve to be humiliated nor rejected.

In the summer of nineteen eighty-nine, we moved back to Tennessee because my husband had work there. My son seemed to be doing much better and going on with his life. He had rededicated his life to God and was working in his church and with different organizations trying to educate people on the causes and dangers of the Aids virus. The respite only lasted for a few months and then it would be several setbacks until the disease would take its toll on him.

Before the disease prohibited travel, my son returned to our old church so he could be baptized and rededicate his life to God. He made this long trip because the ministers he contacted in his area would not baptize him because of the Aids. The whole congregation attended the service, showering him with love. God brought him back to his beginnings and his real spiritual home.

My church family and countless friends had prayed constantly for God to heal my son of this terrible disease and I fasted and prayed until I was weak in body, many times, for his healing. Still, in January, nineteen-ninety, my son took a turn for the worse and all hope was gone that he would make it through this critical illness. All of those who loved this wonderful man were devastated. I remember standing at his graveside, asking God, why did you not heal my son? It seemed as if the voice of God spoke to me and said, I did heal him, completely. In that moment, I knew my son had finished his work on earth and was now in Heaven with Jesus.

During the last three years of his life, my son spent all of his energies working to educate people about Aids, ministering and witnessing to all about the love and forgiveness of God. He worked as chaplain of the Aids floor in one hospital in Dallas. He was included in the nineteen, eighty-nine addition of Who's Who in American Christian Leadership, for his work with Aids victims. Through my son's illness, I learned how hateful the world can be and how loving God is. It was a time when anyone with AIDS was an outcast.

Chapter 18

NO PLACE TO RUN

All through the years of my son's sickness and the other tragedies that beset my children, my husband never quit drinking, did not even slow down. Now that we were alone for the first time in our married lives, the physical, mental and emotional abuse escalated to an all time high. It was as though he thought he could get away with more severe assaults on me because there was no one there to see it.

Suddenly, I knew I could not and would not live this way any longer. There were no children for me to care for, no reason to attempt to make a home for a man who seemed to hate the very sight of me. I no longer had a desire to help a man that cared only for himself and his bottle. I left once again, but just like all the other times, my husband had a way of playing on my sympathy and I knew I could not run from my problems, for there was no place to run. Subsequently, I agreed to return to our home if he promised to quit drinking completely and forever. He entered yet another treatment center and after his treatments were finished this time, it seemed his hard drinking days were over. As usual, he came home with a bottle of pills. The demon of alcohol finally put to rest, but the devils in the pills had come to stay. From that time on, he never took another drink, but his dependence on prescription drugs would live with both of us until the end.

Our world is full of people like my husband, addicted and dependent. Our society has helped to create them. We are proscribed pills that purport to ease every type of problem. We are convinced that our deficiencies and our weaknesses are not our fault; we accept that we are victims. Life expects too much. Life hurts too much. Playing by the rules is too hard. Decency, honor and respect are old-fashioned concepts. No matter what the difficulty, there is a pill to fix it. A pill to make us sleep; a pill to wake us up; a pill to calm our nerves; a pill to still our anger; a pill to get us high; a pill to bring us down. We are no longer responsible for our actions. We are just *sick*, our deeds are a result of things done to us, and we are free from blame.

I have read the Bible through and through. I have not found one place where God condemned any that were sick. However, he did, condemn sinners. The murderer, the thief, the adulterer, the fornicator, the liar, the drunkard, the idolater, whether it was an image, or money, or drugs that was worshiped before him. All the addictions of life, according to the world, go something like this. Society calls it sickness and preachers call it a generational curse. However, God calls it Sin. Therefore, we are all guilty. There is only one way to rid ourselves of that guilt, and that is in a relationship with Jesus Christ.

He offers a cure for the ailments that beset our minds and hearts. All we have to do is have faith and trust in him. The only addiction, this medicine causes, is dependence on the only one who can really ease our problems and give us peace. Even though the environments we live in as a child, affect us, we do not have to live under the curse of the sins of our fathers. Jesus came to give us abundant Life. He died to break the curse of all sin and he turns no one away who call on him for forgiveness.

Chapter 19

WHO IS TO BLAME

Where does the fault lie? Why did our children suffer so much heartache and misery? All of our children had grown up in the church. They attended Sunday school, worship service, Bible school and Christian youth camps. They heard the word of God almost every day. They knew right from wrong. So what happened? I knew the answer, painful as it was; it takes two parents, in one accord, to instill Godly values in a child.

The Bible teaches that a husband should be head of his household and the wife should be his helpmate, not his house cleaner or doormat. He should train up his children in the ways of God and set a good example for them to follow. Jesus said, I can do nothing but what I see my father do. If this was true for the Son of God, how much more meaning does it have for parents of today? If the parental precepts God set forth in the Bible, be ignored only trouble follows.

Was my alcoholic husband solely to blame? Doctors say alcoholism is an illness and the tendency toward alcoholic behavior inherited. My husband left a broken and dysfunctional home at age 13 and raised himself. Is the blame for my children's unhappy lives to rest on my shoulders alone? Did my tormented childhood leave me so weak and afraid that it kept me in such an unhappy situation? Was my stubborn refusal to give up on my marriage and possible salvation of my husband the cause of their problems? Did I misinterpret what God said a wife's duty should be? Was that the bases of our children's wasted lives?

I have no answers for these questions. We are all products of our childhoods. There is, however, a time when we must all take responsibility for our own choices, our own decisions and our own actions. If we spend our time turned around, looking at the past and pointing fingers, then we cannot look to the future. I agree that my children deserved a better childhood. So did my husband, so did I and I believe that our parents deserved better. Where does the blame stop? If at some point you do not take responsibility for your own life, you will have to relive the mistakes of others. If all the blame lies with someone else, getting into Heaven would be a snap, whatever you do is not your fault.

God saved me in nineteen sixty-five and the one happiest for me, was my husband. He was glad that God had come into my life and changed me. He was glad to see my temper controlled, and that my words were cleaner. He was glad that I was taking our kids to church and he made sure they could attend youth camps and such. However, nothing I did, nor the changes God brought about in me, made an impact on him. My prayers and those of others passed right over him. While he was glad for me, he thought he was just fine the way he was. That church stuff was not for him. Those sentiments remained true until he was seventy years old and God brought him up short with a message he could not ignore. *To be explained later!*

If I had made my husband stand on his own two feet and not let him come back into my life repeatedly, without proof he had changed, I might have sped up his salvation, rather than hinder it; if I had stepped out of God's way, he might have been saved many years before he was. I might have saved our boys and girls from the pain and sorrow they brought into their own lives, as they grew older. I have asked these questions of myself for years and I will probably continue to do so. I will probably never know the answer, not in this life anyway.

My life and marriage should not be an example to anyone. Suffering is not an example of anything but suffering. If my life is a lesson, in any way, it is to teach individuals to pray hard and consider well, before marriage and to study the words of God about divorce before entering into one. God will always lead us in the right direction if we trust him. He will always protect and guide us through the dark places of life. Jesus said be not unequally yoked together with unbelievers. That means in marriage, business, or any other relationship in our lives.

If I could go back, would I do things differently? Of course, I would. However, as I look back on it all, I see things that I might not have had to endure. Things that were not God's will for me to endure, had I made the right decision, as I faced each trial. Back then, I had a long way to go and a lot to learn in this school of life and I am taking test every day. I have not yet made it to graduation! We can change nothing in our past. We can endeavor with all of our strength and faith, to do it right the first time.

Chapter 20

THE KIDS

Relating the events between nineteen seventy-two, and two thousand-six becomes a chronicle of horror stories in our lives and in our country.

The Seventies would end the Vietnam War, sending thousands of veterans home to deal with the traumas of that war. We had the Watergate scandal that would cause the resigning of our President. The Eighties would bring in the Church Scandals and the Aids Epidemic.

The Nineties would bring Ice Storms, Hurricanes, and Natural Disasters. It would also be a time of Terrorist Attacks on our government buildings, The World Trade Center in1993, and the Oklahoma bombing in 1995.

The turn of the century 2000, would be like a roller coaster of calamities also; with the terrorist attack on New York City 9-11-2001 that would make the previous bombings look like a child's game in comparison. This act of terrorism would send America into another drawn out and costly war. Then we had the Wall Street Crises and the School Shootings that have left families with nightmares.

For my family, it would be a time of illness, hardships and a near death experience for me. Two-thousand-four, would find me in a hospital on an operating table undergoing heart surgery, while friends from around the world would pray me from death's door.

By 2006, my husband would become very ill also. He would be in the hospital with severe heart failure and facing high-risk surgery. God's light finally went on in his head. For the first time in our married lives, we prayed together and he confessed the Lord Jesus. After his release from the hospital, we went directly to the church to give thanks to God for the miracles he had given us. However, a short time later, the doctors would find cancer in my husband's lungs and for the next few months, it would take its toll on his body, and cause more pain for our family.

The stories of my kids during these times are theirs to tell or keep to themselves. I write my story here hoping that what I learned will help others not to make the same mistakes my husband and I, and eventually our kids, made.

Our children witnessed domestic violence, drunkenness, cursing, and double standards all of their lives. On one side, they heard the Gospel of salvation; on the other side, they heard the opposite. They had to move from place to place, town to town, state to state until they found no roots to grow from. They were shamed until their self-esteem lowered. They made friends and lost friends until they gave up on friends. They suffered disappointments until they lost faith in everything around them. They became run-a-ways, hoping to find something better, only to find more heartaches. They turned to alcohol, drugs and the world, because they could not understand how God could allow these things to be. This is the results of raising children in a dysfunctional and divided home. In the case of my children, it would take years of broken hearts, broken homes, broken lives and unbelievable heartaches and destruction. For some of them it would take a journey through drugs, alcohol, jails, prisons, loss of children and countless days and nights of worry, before their faith in God could live again.

My oldest son ran away when he was seventeen. He carried with him painful emotional scars and memories. The peace he sought all of his life came only in death. Our youngest son shot himself in the face while playing Russian roulette with a loaded gun. My youngest daughter would fight a long battle with alcohol, drugs and suicidal attempts, trying to ease the pain. I walked through my own daughter's blood trying to save her after she had slashed both wrists. With my clothes soaked, blood splattered on the walls and pooled on the floor, I thought she would die before I could get help. Once again, God was there and it was only by his mercy that she lived. I walked miles of floors, stayed up countless nights, cried rivers of tears, and suffered the agony of fear, because I did not know when the call would come that one of them had died.

I rejoice today in knowing that most of my children have found their way back to God. Almost all of them have finished their education. Some are born again Christians and serving the Lord. Most of them have reunited with their children and reconciled with each other. Their road has been long and hard.

However, my list of woes and pain is nothing compared to so many, many others. For all of the pain in my life, I feel that God has blessed me without measure. I lost my firstborn to a deadly disease, but I did not lose my whole family to an epidemic or natural disaster. I have never been homeless. I never had to face an enemy on a battlefield. I was never forsaken or unloved. God gave me the greatest of all gifts, his love and forgiveness.

I give thanks for all the times and ways that God has protected my children. I give thanks in knowing that God saved my husband in the last days of his life. My heart fills with joy when I see my son, who had been out of control due to alcohol abuse and had shot himself while drunk, has found his way back to God and is living a Godly life and trying to teach his children the ways of the Lord. I praise God for my daughter who was so addicted to prescription drugs and alcohol that she tried to kill herself more than once, but is now working in God's Kingdom, trying to help other broken people come to Jesus for deliverance. I thank God that my other daughter has conquered the storms and trials of her life and is now working at making a better life for herself and her family. God has worked his miracles in the lives of my children. I am grateful to see how he is turning the curse into blessings. With God's Grace, we survived all of these troubles and we hope we have learned from past mistakes.

Chapter 21

THE GRANDCHILDREN

The same cycle of addiction and violence that affected their parents; now affects the new generation. At the time of this writing, I have eighteen grandchildren and eight great grands. Some are grown and some still in their early teens, some are still toddlers and the danger signs are evident. I am truly frightened for them, as they try to make their way in this world. In truth, I am scared to death for them and all of the other young people in this country and in the world, since this world is more evil than ever before.

As with older folks, I too yearn for my younger days, not to be young again, but to be in an era governed by decency and principles. I know that change is necessary and inevitable, however, the changes that I see and I am not alone in my opinion, are not for the better.

The parents of today seem not to understand their job description. They are parents, roll models, charged to give love and guidance and exercise discipline when necessary to keep the child going in the right direction. God did not intend for parents to ignore their responsibilities by trying to be best friends with their children. After all, the parent is supposed to be the adult in the relationship. The parent is responsible for the child. The parent should not succumb to the idea that the child will not love him or her if they act like a real parent. God did not want a parent to buy off their child with gifts and permissiveness to assuage their own feelings of guilt and inadequacy.

Our young people are seduced by the media advertising, selling everything under the sun. There is no privacy of person or thought. Children learn about perspiration, menstruation, contraception, tooth whiting, sex stimulates, bras that enhance sexual attractiveness and anything else that will make a buck for someone. The ads do not expound on the products or services that will make you a better person, nor do they encourage morality, modesty or self-control. The advertising moguls say they only advertise the products that sell. Not true. Successful advertising is ahead of the market. It tells the consumer what they need or must have.

The entertainment industry has promoted movies, music and videos that reek of violence, pornography, racisms, hatred and sexual promiscuity, until this generation of young people are confused and have not a clue that it is wrong for them to indulge in these ungodly things. These days, if a young girl tries to hold on to her purity, if she desires to stay a virgin until she marries, then she is a prude. Our children no longer have to buy a ticket and go out to the movies in order to watch all of God's commandments broken in a two-hour script. They can stay at home and watch it all on television, games and the Internet. They can even pull it up on their cell phones. They can see all the filth of Hollywood printed on covers of tabloids and magazines at any checkout counter in most stores in this country.

The minds of our children corrupted, by the shameless nakedness of this generation's celebrities. They can see murder, rape, adultery, fornication, lying, cheating, stealing, racism, hatred, nakedness, and every type of evil known to man acted out on the soap opera. Most parents entertain this kind of filth in their own home, while their children are playing around their feet, hearing the profanity and seeing the acts of violence and immoralities on the screen. Schools pass out condoms and birth control pills to our children. They are sending the message that it is all right to be sexually active as long as you just take precautions. A teenage girl can have an abortion without her parent's knowledge or consent. There is something very wrong with this picture.

We, as God's people, need to wake up to what is happening here. God did not ordain Washington D.C, the C.P.S. or the government to raise our children. He did not call the preacher or teacher to train-up a child in the way he/she should go. He gave that privilege to the parents. There are millions of good, loving parents trying to raise their children to be decent, honest and God fearing. They go to church with their children. They teach their youngsters that God's law is law. They try to instill morals and ethics into their child. Then, these good parents, must send their, good children, to public schools; schools, where love of God, country and fellow man have been legislated out of existence, where honor and values are just words, where being called a good kid is a put down; where young people don't know what immodesty means, because they don't know what modesty is.

Our legislators and courts seem to have forgotten that people who loved God and believed what he said founded this country on God's laws, and Biblical principles. These principles are timeless and are just as relevant today as thousands of years ago. The law of God works!

Our country is governed under a democratic ideology. One percept of a democratic form of government is the protection of the rights of the minority, but the majority rules, not anymore.

The Godless minority rules the Religious majority. Why? It is because we have neglected our rights. We have allowed laws to pass that are in direct opposition to God's laws. We have elected men and women who are more interested in re-election than good government. We have surrendered our country's legacy. We stood back and allowed reverence for God and respect for our country abolished from the schools, public buildings and thoroughfares. The sad thing is that while crosses are no longer in view, and prayer is now an archaic practice, the Godly beliefs of our founding fathers are visible on every historic document and historic building in our country. Our Supreme Court continues to make new laws rather than interpret what our constitution says.

Our constitution, contrary to court opinion, denies the state the right to create a state religion or force participation in it. Nowhere did the forgers of this document deny this country's citizenry the right to honor the Lord God in public, in whatever religious practice was theirs. Those that constructed these historic documents put in writing their belief in the existence of God and this new country's dependence on him. They wrote their desire to build a country free from religious intolerance, but the law of God was to be the law of the land. We have given away their dream. We have allowed our country to become an abomination, a cesspool. The stench of which must offend the nostrils of God.

I love my country and I am proud to be an American. I thank God that I am part of this wonderful land. My patriotism does not preclude my heart felt concern for the future of this country. When we allowed references to God and his law chiseled out of public buildings; removed from our schools and gathering places, we lost the protection of the very God that we permitted to be taken out. We have begun the decline that is making the description America an insult and Christian a joke. Our Heavenly father gave his son for our salvation, for the salvation of every soul in the world. Can we not at least do our best to live by his teachings; abide by his laws? To rebuild our land by the blueprints given us by the framers of this country, based on God's commandments. What is wrong if Thou shalt not kill hangs on the wall of our schools?

I titled this chapter *Grandchildren* as I was thinking of my own grandchildren, but as I write, I realized that all grandchildren are at risk, very terrible risk and I am concerned for all of them. If I have any advice for our young people, it would be to get right with God in their youth; he is the only one who can satisfy the cravings of the souls of humanity.

Drugs/alcohol are killers, but before they kill, they will take away everything in life that one holds dear and will cause people to do things that they never thought possible for them to do.

I have already mentioned the heartaches, trials and hardships that my family endured because of drugs and alcohol. Except for alcohol, all the drugs that my husband ever took came from doctors prescriptions. I am not saying here that all doctors are wrong in prescribing drugs to treat patients for their sickness. However, I am saying that there are doctors, who give out pills, when pills are not necessary and then people get addicted to the pills and the latter state of that person is worse than the first. Then the whole family has to suffer the consequences. I thank God that he can bring deliverance to troubled souls and he can do it without pills. God sacrificed his son to pay for sin so that we may be with him for eternity. When we are young, the idea of eternity is beyond our understanding, but Jesus promises an eternity of glory for those who abide by God's laws. Everything must be paid for, everything. Do not make the price to be paid, too high.

To mothers and fathers, I would say this! Take care to train your children in the ways of God. In the world we live in today, if we do not take control of our own then someone else will. We need to be very careful what we do and what we say and how we live in the presence of our children. Because they say what they hear and do what they see, and the world out there has no mercy on them.

If our country continues on its present course, things will only get worse. We must pray for revival in our churches. We must allow God's Holy Spirit to work in us and we must be willing to go into the highways and hedges and bid the lost to come in, no matter what color, culture, race or what depths of sin we find them. The Church of the living God must unite in one accord, in order to be a light to the world. Jesus said a house divided could not stand. We need to learn how to love our neighbor as ourselves the way God commanded us to do. We need to learn to love ourselves first. That means self-respect, principles, integrity and godliness. God loved us more than we can ever comprehend. Could we send our son to a cross, turn our face away from his suffering, and let him die for a world that would hate the very mention of his name? I think not! We have church buildings on most every block of every city in this country, with pews filled with people whose names are written on the books, but still do not know Jesus, while millions are on their way to hell because we fail to show them there is a better way. God help us to become what he called us to be, fishers of men.

I am amazed at how Judas could have sold our Lord out for a few peaces of silver, but I am more amazed at how people today are still selling him out for less. Some of the mainstream churches are selling him out, rewriting the Holy Bible to make it say what they want it to say. The world has crept into the churches, until the sinners cannot tell the Christians from themselves. We dress like the world, talk like the world, smell like the world and act like the world. We have made idols of everything from sports to movie stars. When our children asked for heroes, we gave them movie stars and athletes.

Jesus said, as it was in the days of Noah; as it was in the days of Lot, so should it be when he comes back. In Genesis 6:5, *we read, "And God saw that the wickedness of man was great in the earth and every imagination of the thoughts of his heart was only evil continually.* I believe those words aptly describe what is happening here. I would advise every one to be prepared for His coming; surely, it cannot be far away.

Chapter 22

NEW BEGINNINGS

My husband passed away two days after Christmas, 2007. I had sat helplessly by his bedside, day and night and prayed for him. I knew God had forgiven him for the long years of his wasted life and that I had forgiven him a long time ago. I still marvel at God's amazing grace that caught him just in time. By then I was physically, emotionally and spiritually exhausted, with not a clue as to what I would do next. I was spending my time on the computer, writing little things for my Website, visiting the Public Library, just killing time, trying to deal with the changes in my life.

In the past few years, I had spent very little time with my oldest daughter who lived in another state. She and her husband thought I needed a change so I decided to move to Texas to be near them. It was a good move for me. As I walked one-step at a time, God began to bring healing to my tired body and weary soul. Except now, I was falling into the same old rut. I was doing the same *nothings*; I was just doing them in Texas instead of Tennessee.

I was now in the year 2008, knowing I wanted to do something for God, who had brought me through so much terrible pain and hardships. No longer young, I asked myself, what could I do now? God found in his will yet another blessing for me and in his goodness, he would let me know that he still had plans for me. He would bring into my life a most wonderful man who would become my best friend and then so much more.

I was always very skeptical and afraid of the Internet. I advised my grandchildren against chatting with strangers on dating sites and that sort of thing. Then one day my son told me, "Mother, you need to go online and make some friends. I said, "Oh, I could not do that, there is no telling what I might get into on there. However, my son helped me set up a profile on a Christian fellowship site where I was able to make a lot of new friends and share God's love. I began to look forward to chatting with my Internet friends. It was there that I met Don Buckel, an ordained minister of the gospel of Jesus Christ. We became friends right away.

Don had lost his wife of more than fifty-two years. He had come from a perfect marriage and had raised three beautiful daughters. He was having a very hard time adjusting to his loss. When we met, we were both in the middle of our grief, loneliness and uncertainties as how to go on with our lives. God is so much wiser than we are. He took us by the hand and led us to each other, because he knew that we could serve him better if he gave meaning to our lives again.

After a few weeks of chatting on the Internet and many phone calls later, Don flew to Dallas to meet my family and me. We had a few days to get to know each other, then Don flew back to his home in California; we continued to talk by phone and e-mails. Then we decided that I needed to come to California to meet his family and friends. December twenty, would find me stepping off my first airplane trip to a waiting Don Buckel.

He proposed to me on Christmas Day. After many emails, phone calls and visits back and forth from Texas to California, we were married in a beautiful wedding ceremony on February 20, two thousand-nine. My wedding present was a seven-day cruise to the Mexican Riviera, aboard a beautiful ship. It was my first time, ever, to be on a ship and I was awestricken at the beauty of the ocean.

We returned to our home in California for a few weeks and then set out to finish our honeymoon on the road, traveling in Don's motor home. We covered all the states from California through Arizona, New Mexico, Texas, Tennessee, Arkansas, Oklahoma and Missouri. We had a wonderful time basking in God's blessings and enjoying the beauty of his creations.

The rolling hills, mountains, plains and deserts were a remarkable sight! I had never done much traveling, so most of the sights were all new to me, and I guess Don got a thrill out of showing me around and this country girl from the Mississippi Delta was in a dreamy wonderland.

We had just started out on our travels, leaving the beautiful mountains of California; we were soon in the desert of Arizona. Don had to do all of the driving, as I was terrified of the roads with all the hills, hairpin curves, cliffs and canyons. We were on our way to visit some friends in Arizona, when he became tired and said he was going to pull over and take a nap. He pulled into the parking lot of a truck stop, and fell asleep. Well, I thought, I will step outside and get some air while he sleeps. About ten minutes later, after walking around this place, I looked up and Don was gone, so was the motor home. I thought to myself, he has left me here all alone, in the desert, where I know not a soul and I was getting very nervous.

I finally found my cell phone; dialed his number and asked him were he was, only to hear him say, I am gone. Long story short, his nap lasted for about ten minutes and when he awoke, thinking I was sleeping in the back of the motor home, he just pulled out and left me. He came back to get me and I was ready to plow into him good, but when I crawled back into the motor home, he was laughing and singing the old song, Hey, good-lookin, whatcha got cookin. I did not stay angry long. However, by the time we returned home after two months on the road, we found that all our family and friends knew the story of Don leaving his bride at a truck stop while on our honeymoon. Don thought he would never live that one down.

Finally, we arrived back home, to begin the rest of our lives together. Suddenly, I found myself in the middle of a new and different world than what I was use to. I now had to adjust to living far away from my family, friends and everything that was familiar to me and my new husband had to deal with trying to help me with all the changes. It would not be easy for him. He, being born and raised in southern California; living here all of his life; being surrounded by life-long friends and all of his family, including his grandchildren, all being Christians, was for me like stepping into another world.

I had lived most of my life in the Deep South, in a completely different lifestyle; dealing with a culture shift and asking myself, what in the world am I doing here? I am sure my husband was asking himself questions as well. When you mix a little Iris/Indian with German, you realize that God has a sense of humor in bringing the two together. Even my cooking habits were alien to him. He was not accustomed to southern dishes like grits, gravy, chicken dumplings and sweet tea.

We passed through our first year together. It had been both wonderful and exciting. I had come to make new friends and becoming friends with his wonderful family was an added blessing.

As we grew closer to each other and closer to God, as we faced trials and concerns for all the changes going on in our Nation and around the world, we endeavored to help where we could. We prayed that our efforts would meet God's will, standards, and most of all, that through our lives and works, we would be able to reach some with the gospel of our Lord and Savior, Jesus Christ.

In 2010, we would take another road trip. This time we would travel by automobile and our route would take us through Arizona and down the California coastline to Oregon, Washington State, Idaho and back through Montana, Wyoming, Utah, Nebraska, to California and home. We were on the road for about seven weeks on this trip. We had fun just driving as long as we felt like it, then stopping to visit new friends and churches on the way. We retuned home to continue our lives together. We attended church regularly and kept up our daily active lives. We were happy and content with the new life we shared. My health had improved and we thanked God every day for the blessings he gave us in each other and our family and friends around us.

Chapter 23

ONE MORE HEARTACHE

I have learned many things in my life, but the most important thing I have learned is that not all of God's blessings are a gift some are just loans. The gifts and callings of God are without repentance, but he does collect on the loans. Therefore, we never know when God's loan of a loved one will come due. We need to be careful to show love to our family and friends because one day God will call them or us back.

In the summer of, 2010, Don felt a rough spot on the side of his tongue. He thought he had chipped a tooth so he made an appointment with his dentist who found nothing amiss. Then he made an appointment with his doctor who found a small growth and sent him to a specialist, who found a small cancer. They removed it quickly and said they got it all, so we did not think about it for a while. A few months later Don discovered a small lump on his neck, so he went back to the specialist who surgically removed this lump and was sure he would be all right. However, a few months later, another lump appeared on his neck. This time he refused surgery, but consented to doing chemo and radiation treatments.

Shortly after Christmas 2011, Don began his treatments while we prayed they would work. He made it through nine treatments and was getting so weak and worn out that he could not function. He refused to take any more treatments because he had no guarantee that the treatments would even help. We decided to start a new diet plan that was supposed to be a cure for cancer. Don spent countless dollars on new foods and gadgets that was to make the plan work. I had to learn all over again how to cut, chop and cook these special dishes. I cooked and prayed with every meal, that God would work a miracle and make this plan work; however, as I watched the cancer grow, I knew it was not going to work. It was like going back in time, and reliving the same episodes of watching someone I loved die all over again. Only this time it would be harder.

My husband was such a strong man and his faith in God was unwavering. He was at peace with knowing he would not live many more days. We had beautiful moments during this time; we talked for hours and spent all the time we could with our family and friends. The grandchildren would come and have fellowship, bringing their guitars and singing the songs Don loved, sharing prayers and communion.

Don made it through, until April 20, two thousand-twelve and passed away peacefully as me and two of his daughters stood by his bedside. My faith in God never weakened and I knew better than to ask God, Why? However, I could not make myself even try to understand why this wonderful man had to pass before me, and I could not look ahead and see a way that I could go on without him. He had been a blessing from God to bring happiness into my troubled life and it took all of God's grace in me to help me walk through that dark valley. I learned the meaning of taking one-step at a time.

I was surrounded by people who loved me, who mourned with me, while they were hurting just as much as I was. I had moments of despair and moments of anger; moments of hopelessness; moments of feeling completely alone. I had people coming and going, saying all the right things to try to ease the pain. When people hovered over me, I just wanted them to leave me alone. Then when they left me alone, I could not stand the loneliness, it was unbearable. There were times when I wanted to scream, this is not fair. I would walk floors, cry and try to figure out where to go and what to do from here. I remembered the words of Job in the Bible, The lord giveth and the lord taketh away, blessed be the name of the lord.

After it was over, we laid Don to rest, and everybody else went back to his or her own lives, I felt like I had no life left. I thought of moving back to my family in Texas or Tennessee; but that meant leaving Don's family and our friends whom I had come to love. I decided to stay put for as long as I could.

At the time of this writing, I am now in the year two thousand-fourteen. It has been more than two years since I lost my husband and no day goes by that I do not miss him. Sometimes I still find myself gazing at the empty chair where he used to sit or missing his smile and the kindness he showered on me. Not one day goes by that I do not wish I could bring him back just to tell him how much I appreciate him. I do not question God's will. I wait for the day when I will see him again, in a place with no cancers, aids or anything else to separate us from the ones we love. God's word says to lay up for ourselves treasures in Heaven, where thieves do not break through and steal. That is what disease is, just a thief that breaks in and steals our bodies. Thank God, for his promise of a new body that is not made of flesh and bones.

As I walk in God's Grace, I have to keep in mind that there is more than one type of Grace. We have redeeming grace, living grace and dying grace. Redeeming grace came with the death of Jesus on the cross. Living grace comes daily as we walk through life's struggles and trials and we learn that his grace is sufficient for every situation that we come into. Dying grace will come at our life's end when Jesus will be there to walk us through that valley, and this grace will not come to us until we get there. We are to live our lives without fear of tomorrow, nor what it might bring. When we lose a loved one, if we know they are right with God, then we can rejoice in knowing that we will be with them again. We need to live life in a way that when we are gone, the ones we leave behind will have good memories. No matter how much wealth or material possessions we leave behind, our loved ones will remember us by the kind of life we lived while on this earth, and those memories could mean the turning of someone else to or from God.

My hope is that I can live a life that is pleasing to my lord and that I might help others to come to Jesus and break the shackles of sin that holds one captive. There is no peace in this life outside of knowing the Prince of Peace.

Chapter 24

POETRY FROM THE HEART

The following chapter will consist of some of the Author's most read and best loved poems. My hope is that they bring encouragement and inspiration to all who read them.

A MILLION MILES AGO

Wind was blowing through my hair, playing softly on my face.
As I skipped along that country road, there on the old home place.
I remember awesome sunsets, as they kissed the day goodnight.
The moon and stars danced together, as they glowed across the sky!

I remember a golden pond, down by the old school,
where we learned to read and write, and how to keep the golden rule.
Where we pledged allegiance to our flag, bowed our heads to pray,
and thanked God for our freedom, to call on Him each day.

I can still hear mother singing, as she worked in those fields.
The breeze would carry her song, to the trees upon the hills.
How she would sing the Rock of Ages, and Do Not Pass Me by.
Songs about the angels, singing far beyond the sky.

I remember foolish thoughts of how I would like to get away,
and explore the world out yonder, beyond the cotton fields and hay.
Now that I have seen it all, and things I wish, I did not know.
I would like to go back a few years and a million miles ago.

Awe, a million miles ago, when I was young and free.
Before my dreams came true, and then shattered at my feet.
Now that I have seen it all; and things I wish I did not know.
I would like to go back a few years, and a million miles ago.

I Remember Mother

I remember her in her cotton dress, apron around her waist.
Cooking in the kitchen, food for every taste.
I remember her in the garden, spade and shovel in her hand,
Mixing up the soil from a dry and crusty land.

I remember her in the doorway, as she waved us off to school.
She was sure to remind us to keep the golden rule.
I remember how hard she worked, at her unending tasks.
Never complaining, and for help she would never ask.

I remember her by the fireplace, in her old rocking chair,
reading the scriptures, about a home so bright and fair.
I remember how she taught us faith, hope, and honesty.
That if we had love one for the other, that is all we would really need.

I remember the day we kissed her, and laid her down to rest.
Then the angels came and took her, to that homeland of the blessed.
I remember the seeds of kindness she sowed along life's way.
I know she is reaping her harvest, in heaven on this day.

DRUGS

She walks through her memories, searching for the good.
Trying to find the answers, wishing she could.
She remembers all her dreams and hopes gone astray.
Her life is now in shambles, and her world blown away.

She thinks back to a time, when at her mother's side.
She learned about Jesus, how he had been crucified.
Her tears began to fall and trickle down her face,
She wondered how she ever got to this awful place.

It did not take much, just one slip at a time.
A little here, a little there and soon she would find.
That with each puff of the drugs her friends gave,
She would need more and more, as her body would crave.

Soon she found another thrill; called ecstasy,
She would try this too; maybe it would set her free.
However, with each little take, it would only bring more pain,
Soon she would take the needle and stick it in her vain.

Just one more high, to help her through this day,
Just one more fix, then her fears would go away.
Nevertheless, no matter what she did, no matter how she tried,
She found that not all the drugs could satisfy.

She heard her mother's voice somewhere from the past.
Telling her, Jesus had a love that would last.
She felt so helpless; she knew she was at the end;
She wondered could he love me in spite of my sins.

She fell down before him, on bended knees.
She prayed for mercy that would make her free.
As he lifted her higher than she'd ever been,
She knew peace at last, and was free from her sin.

BETWEEN NOW AND THEN

When I cross this valley, I will reach my final home.
I will hear the angels singing; look upon God's golden throne.
Someday I will bid farewell to this fleshly coat of sin.
However, I still have a ways to go, between now and then.

I still have mountains yet to climb before I get there.
I have unfinished tasks, Godly things I need to share.
I have troubled days ahead, and trials I hope to win.
I have deserts yet to cross between now and then.

I get discouraged when my world turns upside down.
At times, I get frightened at the evil all around.
I am racing to the finish line; it could be around the next bend.
Just a few more laps to run, between now and then.

I feel my ship sinking as the winds tip my sails,
as I fight for control on life's sea of stormy gales.
Nevertheless, Jesus is my captain until the voyage ends.
I have a few more waves to ride, between now and then.

NOT FAR TO GO

Jesus came to bring freedom to the heart bound in shame.
He came to give peace, found only in His name.
He came to give living waters to the thirsty souls of men.
He came to give abundant life to all who would let Him in.

You do not have to walk alone in the darkness of your night.
You do not have to be afraid of the storms in your sight.
You do not have to remain behind the past's guilty bars.
You do not have far to go, he will meet you where you are.

His grace is sufficient; true to his word he will always be;
Moreover, all his promises are for you, the same as for me.
He said all we need is faith smaller than a grain of sand,
and the mountains before us would move at our command.

It takes one cry of his name for his arms to unfold.
One touch of his hand and you become whole.
Just one drop of his blood will cover all the wounds and scars.
You do not have far to go, he will meet you where you are.

WALKING ON QUICKSAND

If you do not know Jesus and all he has done for you.
If you have denied him and wonder if his words are true.
You need to take a second look back over your life's span.
Find out he is real before you reach the quicksand.

If you have been looking at your troubles, and blinded by the view.
If you hope that fame and fortune awaits you.
If you are walking without faith outside the master's plan.
Just be careful where you step, you are soon to reach the quicksand.

If you do not believe, Jesus came to give everlasting life.
If you are following, the trends of evil that only bring you strife.
If you do not believe that, you are just another fallen man.
Be careful where step, you are now walking on quicksand.

Be careful as you walk; look both ways at crossroads.
Be careful or you will fall beneath sin's heavy load.
Jesus is walking near you; reaching for your hand.
Let him save you, before you reach the quicksand.

HEAVEN'S GATES

I just entered heaven's gates; have not been here very long.
The angels are now singing their new song.
You might be sad since the Lord sent for me,
So I wanted to let you know, I am all right you see!

As I entered Heaven's gates, with an angel guiding me,
the first thing I noticed, from pain I was free.
My eyes no longer failed me; my ears were so clear,
my voice no longer weak; my heart no longer feared.

I walk on golden streets where no sorrow can be known,
and hear a million angels sing, around a golden throne.
As I gaze upon the beauty of what mortal man cannot see,
I am now in God's presence for all eternity.

So, miss me for a while and then let your mind be at peace;
cry a few tears that will bring your heart release.
Then, remember all the good times, we shared along life's way,
and know I will be waiting, when you enter Heaven's Gates.

GLIMPSES

Now and then, I take a stroll down memory lane.
I get a glimpse of things of which I once complained.
Little feet running over floors I had just cleaned,
laughter and tears, playing on my heartstrings.

Toy trains and baby dolls scattered all around;
Spills and squeals and children's playful sound.
I see schoolbooks and homework, and lessons for tests.
PTA meetings, where I reviewed my child's progress.

I get a glimpse of ballgames; of picnics on the river;
Sharing blankets in the sand, as night winds made us shiver.
I see joy and happiness; goodnight kisses on my cheek.
I see a few bad times that made our hearts weep.

Sometimes I grew weary when at a day's end;
my body tired and my mind in a spin.
I looked forward to a day, my babies would be grown,
when my role would be lighter and my time would be my own.

Now as I turn the pages of my picture book.
I get a glimpse of sweetness everywhere I look.
As I recall those moments, my heart swells within.
If I had it in my power, I would make them babies once again.

Therefore, mothers take heed as you hold your baby's hand.
As you, watch their first step, first tooth, and first friend.
Train them up in the ways of God, no matter what others think.
Hold them close to your heart, for time is but a blink.

BENEATH HIS WINGS OF LOVE

As I sail through the clouds in my space on God's land.
I will lean on his promises and hold to his hand.
He will hide me from the storms, beneath his wings of love,
as I keep my ears open to his voice from above.

Beneath his wings of love, I will be safe from all harm.
Though I am tossing in the winds, I will feel no alarm.
As I soar in his goodness and rest in his grace,
From beneath his wings of love, all trials I can face.

Beneath his wings of love, I will find strength that is not my own.
There is a new storm on the horizon, and its destiny unknown.
Even though there is ciaos all around, and the world seems to crash.
I will be hiding in his feathers, when the lightening bolts flash.

Beneath his wings of love, I will find refuge from evil darts.
His grace will be sufficient, when sorrows pierce my heart.
When arrows strike at me, I will be safe as a dove
He will be my fortress, if I am beneath his wings of love.

As You Are

Are you tired of all the pain that you feel?
All the tears you are crying; the wounds that will not heal?
Are dark clouds hanging low, does the sun no longer shine?
Is your ship-sinking, do you feel you are running out of time?

Do your lips no longer smile; have your friends gone astray?
Do you feel lost and alone; that you cannot find your way?
As your eyes search for a lighthouse ore life's raging sea;
Does the fog dim your vision; does no one hear your plea?

You do not have to be rich, famous or well educated!
You do not have to be beautiful, handsome or sophisticated!
He has chosen the weak to confound the wise.
Come to Jesus, as you are; and he your soul will baptize.

SOUND THE TRUMPET

When the humming birds start to fly; hovering low above my head;
When the robin starts to sing and the caterpillar begins to shed.
When the flowers start to bloom; when grass is green on the hills;
When the trees sway in splendor and grain is budding in the fields.

When I smell the scent of rain, as it sprays softly in the breeze.
Then I know spring has come, and has melted winter's tease.
When I look in God's word; read the signs he spoke about.
The world would not stand long, when we leave him out.

When man's thoughts are only evil; when lawlessness rules the land.
When sin eats like a cancer, we know he is coming back again.
Therefore, sound the trumpet at the gates; lift your voice load and clear.
When these things began to happen, our redemption is near.

THAT RECKONING DAY

I remember a time, not far in the past.
We honored marriage and love would last!
Moms and dads could still make the rules;
Teachers could lead prayer in our schools.

We still had family prayer each night.
Fathers taught their children right.
Bedtime stories replaced television.
Families stuck together without division.

The Ten Commandments hung in our halls.
The Lord's Prayer hung on our walls.
Our house was a home, not just a pad.
Our children were thankful for what they had.

We honored our flag and raised it with pride.
We honored our soldiers, and cried if they died.
We worked for our needs, every dollar and cent.
We did not ask handouts from our government.

Since the liberals have changed everything,
Our kids think life is just a game.
We now have a country full of hate and crime.
Human life is not worth a dime.

I wonder what we will do; what will we say,
When it comes that reckoning day?
When God's wrath falls on this nation,
For the sins committed against his creation.

Until We Untie His Hands

If I could wipe the tears from the eyes that cry,
If I could always say hello and never, say good-by.
If I could be a friend, that could hold up the weak.
If I could be an oasis, when shelter someone seeks.

Who could name the stars and hold them in their hand?
Who could move a mountain and count the grains of sand?
Who could run every marathon, and win first prize?
Who could walk on the waters and hold back the tides?

Who could speak a word, and cause all pain to cease?
Who could pick up the fallen man, and give him peace?
Who could find the lost children and bring them all home?
Who could teach the whole world, to sing a love song?

If I could work miracles, I would make the world a better place,
If I could, I would paint a smile on every sad face.
Only Jesus has this power and we need to understand,
That he cannot do his work, until we untie his hands.

GRACE AND MERCY

Mercy found me when I was in despair,
When I was at the end and had no one to care.
Mercy watched over me in my deepest sorrow.
Mercy brought me through yesterday's acts of horror.

Mercy came from above in the shadow of death.
Mercy touched my body, and breathed in me new breath.
Mercy gave me another chance, when I had played my last game.
Grace gave me one more chance, to call on Jesus' name.

Grace caught my vision when I was alone and scared.
Grace waited in the shadows of my dark despair.
Grace picked me up when I stumbled in my strife.
Grace wrote my name on God's book of life.

It is Grace and Mercy that holds my hand each day.
It is Grace and Mercy who keeps me, lest I stray.
It will be Grace and Mercy that takes me safely on.
Because of God's Grace and Mercy, I am never alone.

I MISS YOU

I remember when you left me, and you told me not to cry.
You said you were going to a place, where no one would ever die.
You said you would wait there by the river, where the grass is evergreen.
Where the tree of life is standing, and forever angels sing.

If you're standing on the banks of that clear and crystal sea,
If you're strolling through the meadows with golden dust beneath your feet.
If you're singing in the choir with Heaven's angels around the Throne.
Just keep your eyes upon that Eastern Gate, for soon I'm coming home.

I miss you in the morning, when the sunrise clips the trees.
I miss you in the noonday, when your smile I long to see.
I miss you in the twilight, when the evening shadows fall.
But, every minute of the day, is when I miss you most of all.

"IF I LEAVE"

If in my life, I dropped a seed, of kindness now and then.
That painted a smile on a broken heart, or just grew into a friend.
If you could, look and see God's love, deep inside of me,
The valleys crossed, and the mountains climbed, have won my victory.

If I leave without a warning, without a chance to say, "good-by,"
Do not let your heart be troubled, and tell your eyes not to cry.
Just keep walking on your journey, help someone along the way.
I will meet you in the morning, where all tears are, wiped away.

If you leave without a warning; without a chance to say "good-by,"
My heart would fill with sorrow, and I know my eyes would cry.
I will just keep walking on my journey, in the steps you leave for me,
Then I will meet you in the morning, beside that clear and crystal sea.

LORD, I JUST WANT TO THANK YOU

If I could name all the blessings that to me, mean the most.
If I could pick one from a million, I could not come close.
It would take many pages and more time that I have left.
To name answered prayers for others, not to mention myself.

As I sit here in my thoughts of how many times, I prayed.
All the needs I could not fill, but you somehow found a way.
As I try to find the words to express my gratitude;
Somehow, words are insufficient to give thanks to you.

Therefore, I come to you today, not asking anything.
I just want to say I love you, and give praises to your name.
I thank you for my family and the friends you have given me.
For times I could not stand alone; you picked me up and carried me.

For all the times I fell and forgot, you were there.
You were standing in the shadows, just waiting for my prayers.
I remember the times I cried, my whole self fell apart.
You touched me and healed my broken heart.

I know tomorrow I will come again and stand before your face.
I will bring you all my troubles; ask you to take my place.
I will call out names and things I need for you to do.
However, for now, Lord, I just want to thank you. Amen!

1973

Mae and Bobby 1087

Mae and Don Wed

Mae and Don 2010